THE **HOME**Houseproject

the future
of affordable
housing

edited by David J. Brown

texts by
Steve Badanes
David J. Brown
Ben Nicholson
Michael Sorkin

SOUTHEASTERN CENTER FOR CONTEMPORARY ART

The MIT Press
Cambridge, Massachusetts
London, England

First MIT Press edition, 2004

This book was produced in conjunction with the multiyear initiative The HOME House Project with two exhibitions at the Southeastern Center for Contemporary Art (SECCA), May 9–July 6, 2003 and October 18–April 3, 2004.

Southeastern Center for Contemporary Art
750 Marguerite Drive, Winston-Salem, NC 27106
Tel: (336) 725-1904
Fax: (336) 722-6059
Web: secca.org

The MIT Press
Five Cambridge Center, Cambridge, MA 02142-1493
Tel: (800) 405-1619
Fax: (800) 406-9145
Web: mitpress.mit.edu

MIT Press books may be purchased at special quantity discounts for business or sales promotional use. For information, please Email special_sales@mitpress.mit.edu or write to Special Sales Department, The MIT Press, 5 Cambridge Center, Cambridge, MA 02142.

Habitat for Humanity data courtesy of Habitat for Humanity International

Text Editor: Nancy Margolis
Design & Typography: Kevin France
This book was set in Mrs. Eaves, Simian Display, Trade Gothic and was printed and bound in the United States.
Cover: Adaptive Reuse by Steven Raike, page 72

Exhibition venues:

The University of North Texas Art Gallery, Denton, Texas
(April 8–May 25, 2004)

The Contemporary Art Center of Virginia, Virginia Beach, Virginia
(June 13–July 14, 2004)

The Neighborhood Housing Services of Asheville
in collaboration with the Asheville Art Museum,
Green Building Council, and others,
Asheville, North Carolina
(September 17–October 31, 2004)

Center for Visual Art and Culture
University of Maryland, Baltimore County, Baltimore, Maryland
(September 30–November 30, 2004)

El Paso Museum of Art, El Paso, Texas
(April 24–August 14, 2005)

Museum of Design, Atlanta, Georgia
(January 16–April 15, 2006)

Weisman Art Museum, Minneapolis, Minnesota
(February 4–April 30, 2006)

Library of Congress Cataloging-in-Publication Data

The HOME House Project: the future of affordable housing / edited by David J. Brown ; texts by Steve Badanes ... [et al.].—1st MIT Press ed.
     p.   cm.
  Includes catalog of two exhibitions at the Southeastern Center for Contemporary Art, May 9–July 6, 2003 and Oct. 18–Apr. 3, 2004.
  ISBN 0-262-52432-5 (pbk.)
1. Public housing—United States—Exhibitions. 2. Architecture, Domestic—United States—Designs and plans—Exhibitions.
3. Architecture—Environmental aspects—Exhibitions. 4. Architecture, Domestic—Competitions—Exhibitions.
5. HOME House Project—Exhibitions.
I. Brown, David J., 1952– II. Badanes, Steven. III. Southeastern Center for Contemporary Art.

NA7540.H66 2004
728'.1' 07473—dc22
                                                                                                    2004021309

10 9 8 7 6 5 4 3 2 1

Acknowledgments

The HOME House Project is an enormous undertaking and would not have been possible without the input, dedication, and generosity of many people and organizations and all of them deserve my most sincere regards and respect. Foremost, I wish to graciously thank SECCA Executive Director Vicki Kopf, the entire SECCA board and staff for their unwavering support in all areas of the project. Terri Dowell-Dennis and Mark Linga added valuable insight and critical comments through the planning stages and created a range of programs that helped open many doors to the understanding of sustainable design and those who have made great contributions in the field. Angie Debnam handled the too-many headaches of registration for the more than 800 applicants from around the world. I thank her for constantly updating what seemed to be an endless list. Josh Rickards and Lyndon Bray headed a crew of art handlers (Neal Goode, Eric Jackson, Andrew Schultheis, Joe Morgan, Laura Lashley, and John Blackburn) in designing, installing, packing, and crating the huge volume of works that were displayed two different times in two formats. Amy Garland deserves great praise for creatively getting the word out. Additional assistance was graciously supplied by Karin Burnette, Alyson Watts, Maggie Morrison, Susan Boone, David Mooneyham, and interns Moire Beauchamp, Jessica Roland, and Emily Johnson. Kevin France did a marvelous job of sifting through and rearranging a horde of data in designing this special publication.

Michael Sorkin, Steve Badanes, and Ben Nicholson are incredible individuals with too many attributes between them to list here (please see their bios at the end of the book). I first met Mr. Badanes twenty years ago and since then have watched and listened to his remarkable journey and uncommon wisdom. As jurors of the 25 Awards of Merit and as contributors to this book, their expertise, insight, and camaraderie evidenced a deep understanding of the possibilities of art and architecture to responsibly address a deep-rooted social problem that affects us all.

R. Phillip Hanes, Jr. and his associate Chris Griffith became early champions of the project and began to sing its praises around the country. I am in their debt for believing, thinking big, and bringing forward Millard and Linda Fuller, founders of Habitat for Humanity; Thomas Lovejoy and Anne Hummer of the H. John Heinz III Center for Science, Economics, and the Environment, and many others. Although this project is independent of Habitat for Humanity, I am indebted to Neville Eastwood of Habitat International for his active support and for allowing us to use their data in this project. For the City of Winston-Salem, I wish to applaud the Honorable Mayor Allen Joines;

Dr. Monica Lett, Executive Director, Community and Neighborhood Programs; Terri Beckman and Paula McCoy, L.I.S.C.; Mel White, Old Salem; Lisa Yewdall, Southside CDC; and Habitat for Humanity, Forsyth County. Bill Benton and Bud Baker have exhibited a thoughtful vision by teaming together in an ambitious effort to build five of the houses in the city. In other parts of the country, I appreciate all that you have done to make the project of vital interest in your particular community. In Denton, Texas: Diana Block and Sara-Jayne Parsons, University of North Texas Art Gallery. Virginia Beach, Virginia: L. Cameron Kitchin, Brenda LaBier, and Ragan Cole-Cunningham, Contemporary Art Center of Virginia. Asheville, North Carolina: Hedy Fischer and Randy Shull; H. Christopher Slusher, Beth Carter, Clay Estep, Neighborhood Housing Services of Asheville; Pam Myers, Asheville Art Museum; Ken Czarnomski, Asheville Buncombe Technical Community College; Brenda Coates, Mary Godfrey; Boone Guyton, Traci Kearns, Maggie Leslie, Green Building Council; Richard Fort, and Linda Fowler. Baltimore: Symnes Garder, David Yeager, and Renee van der Stelt, Center for Visual Arts and Culture, University of Maryland, Baltimore County; Marc Cameron, Neighborhood Design Center; American Institute of Architects, Baltimore chapter. Atlanta: Angelyn S. Chandler, Museum of Design. El Paso: Becky Duval-Reese, Christian Gerstheimer, and Amy V. Grimm, El Paso Museum of Art; Lyndel King and Colleen Sheehy, Weisman Art Museum, along with Thomas Fisher, Dean of the College of Architecture and Landscape Architecture at the University of Minnesota and the Minnesota Chapter of the American Institute of Architects.

Jane Milner, Executive Director of the Housing Partnership of Winston-Salem/Forsyth County, Incorporated courageously stepped forward at the beginning of the project to express her support by agreeing to build the first of several houses. Please applaud Forsyth Technical Community College, Dr. Gary M. Green, President; Cynthia Bioteau, Vice-President, Darrell H. Hill, Dean Engineering Division, Herb Burns, Department Chair, Architectural Construction Technology Department, as well as a group of dedicated students and faculty for working together to build the first house. Because of their involvement with the HOME House Project, the school is targeting sustainable, affordable design and construction to help chart its future. Also from Forsyth Tech, I commend the following: Architectural Technology Program Instructor William M. Marion, students: Daniel Alexander, Chad Cornatzer, Valerie Gordy, Jake Groce, Robert Hampton, Pam Harmon, Charles Hauck, David Martin, Margaret Pishner, Cody Smith, Mat Tesh, David Warren; Landscape Horticluture Program Coordinator Roger Richardson, students: Thomas Gammons, Wendel Love, Matt Noyes, Lisa Swarthout; Carpentry Program Coordinator Odell Grose; Plumbing Program Coordinator Ike

Brown; Heating Air Conditioning and Refrigeration Program Coordinator Dwight Cornelison; Electrical/Electronics Technology Program Coordinator Ken Hanes and his students.

Others that lent generous assistance at pivotal points in the project include Suzanne Fetscher, Nathan Wieler, Mardi Oakes, Jeff Pettus and Vicki Vitiello, George Thorn and Nello McDaniel, Nancy Crown, Walter David, Becky Hannum, and Rai Glover, Allison Arieff, Bryan Bell, Howard Decker, Lira Luis, Rick Douglas, Katherine Christie, Lou Adkins, and especially my family (Krystyna Puc and Zak) for their continued love and support. Due to the nature of this on-going initiative, I am happy to report that the HOME House Project community continues to gain individual and organizational partners on an almost daily basis.

Please join me in thanking the following organizations and foundations for their generous support. Today, projects such as this can only be realized with additional outside funding. Thanks to all of you for allowing us to follow our ambitious plans.

- This project is supported in part by an award from The National Endowment for the Arts, which believes that a great nation deserves great art.
- Additional support was received from The North Carolina Arts Council, an agency funded by the State of North Carolina and the National Endowment for the Arts and The Wallace-Foundation Funds
- The Elizabeth Firestone Graham Foundation
- An anonymous donor
- Bank of America (for the design awards)

Lastly, it has been an honor to galvanize the creative force of all the artists, designers, and architects who spent enormous amounts of time and thought in realizing the large range of ideas that are pushing affordable housing to new and healthy levels. I raise a glass of gratitude to all of you and encourage you to continue what you have so wonderfully started.

djb

NATIONAL ENDOWMENT FOR THE ARTS

www.ncarts.org

Bank of America

CONTENTS

Houses are the great paramour for architects, from the most successful all the way down to the most struggling. We draw them on the backs of napkins. Too often, when I look at what builders and developers are doing, we're not talking about architecture any longer. We're talking about capitalism at its most obscene. The public has bought into the mediocrity and insipid attitude of manufactured and spec houses, and has given up any hope of creating homes with spirit.

Samuel Mockbee

Philippe Barrier
Philippe Barrier Collective
Lawrence, Kansas

Introduction

The HOME House Project, the future of affordable housing is an evolution of the Southeastern Center for Contemporary Art's *Artist and the Community* series. Begun in 1994, *Artist and the Community* has focused on issues and aspects of life in Winston-Salem—from industry to history, education, and social welfare. *Artist and the Community* artists have built interactive relationships with community members, thus expanding the understanding of contemporary art while forging innovative ties with local cultural, educational, and civic organizations.

Although many of the *Artist and the Community* projects have been highly successful, the HOME House Project has demonstrated unusual potential for significant impact. By encouraging the merging of outstanding design with the responsible use of sustainable materials and technologies, this project has the ability to affect the future of affordable housing and to minimize the stigma often associated with it.

Even before a single house has been built, the response to this initiative has been overwhelming. One can only imagine the impact on the field of affordable housing as the designs begin to pop up in neighborhoods all across the United States and beyond. A bright new future for affordable housing is before us, and SECCA is pleased to be playing a part in this evolution.

None of this would have been possible without first the innovative idea of David J. Brown, senior curator at SECCA. David is to be commended not only for the concept of the HOME House Project, but for his unwavering dedication and resolve to bring his ideas to fruition. The support of the entire SECCA staff and board of directors is also greatly appreciated. We are all waiting to see the revolution begin.

Vicki Kopf
Executive Director

Michael Sorkin

According to estimates, over a billion and half people around the world lack a decent place to live. Although America has higher housing standards than the rest of the world and a lower percentage of population that is ill-housed, we still struggle to provide shelter for our poor. Our city streets are filled with homeless. Our ghettoes persist and now stretch into the suburbs. The destruction of post-war housing projects proceeds apace, their former tenants left to fend for themselves in an unsympathetic market. According to the last census, approximately seven million housing units in America have severe to moderate "physical problems."

Added to this is America's growing contempt for its unfortunate. This mean-spiritedness has roots both in America's historic culture of self-reliance and in the racism that has long dogged our sense of responsibility to the poor. Ronald Reagan's rants against fictionalized "welfare queens" taking advantage of our *richesse oblige*, neo-liberal programs (both here and abroad) foisting "autonomy" on those who have no resources to attain it, the virtual disappearance of federal aid for housing construction, the continued impotence of market-based solutions, and the general neglect of the public sphere—the famous "bowling alone" syndrome—have all contributed to the crisis.

In addition, dramatic increases in labor mobility have created a culture of impermanence that vitiates the very idea of home. The average American worker is obliged to relocate constantly in pursuit of jobs, gone to non-union states or outsourced abroad. Indeed, even retirement is, for many, a time of mobility; witness the thousands of elderly living nomadic lives in their Winnebagos. They join the millions who live in the immobilized condition of the "mobile" home, our miserable contribution to the manufactured housing industry, the best our culture has been able to produce in the way of high-volume, low-cost housing.

There is a mismatch between our existing housing stock and those seeking homes. Now that the nuclear family is no longer our primary living arrangement, our fixation on the single-family dwelling is less and less appropriate. Indeed, the traditional family now accounts for less than half the households in America, and that share continues to shrink. The single-family dwelling simply cannot meet the requirements of our burgeoning diversity of living arrangements—single-parent households, dual-income families, and a wide variety of both contractions and expansions of households. Like generals, though, architects and builders continue to fight the last war, designing for a world that no longer exists. Where, then, are we to call home?

Housing is at the core of both our comfort and of our political life: We are where we live. From the earliest days of the republic, this link has been critical to the idea of American freedom. The connection begins with the definition of citizenship, the set of privileges and responsibilities that establish a citizen's value. Citizenship is thus itself a kind of "house"—a political envelope that defines both our freedom of action and our sense of our own limits. The dimensions of the private sphere enable our participation in the public realm. These dimensions are established in a dialogue between self-aggrandizement and altruism: democracy is an ongoing negotiation between citizens and state over the limits of personal freedom and of mutual obligation. We tend to regard this negotiation as a conflict, a zero-sum game.

When we negotiate, we speak in terms of our "rights." The inalienability of such rights is what a citizen has as a negotiating counter in democracy, forming the basis of his or her claim for space. The Declaration of Independence enshrines a particular set of rights—life, liberty, the pursuit of happiness—and the Constitution and its legal ramifications establish others, including basic freedoms and derivative rights like gun ownership or women's control of their bodies. These rights are the point of departure for the larger negotiation over the precise shape of our individual possibilities. And for centuries now, these rights have been intimately bound up with the idea of property. Indeed, it has been the ownership of property that has been the primary medium for establishing not simply the extent of citizenship, but its very fact. Although we no longer require landholding for voting privileges, the notional connection between property and citizenship is strong.

And yet politically – despite our fealty to property - we do not recognize the right to shelter as fundamental. In the endless conversation about the meaning of liberty in the variety of political systems that purport to provide it, there has been a historic divide between those political systems that regard the state as responsible for providing necessities (food, shelter, and medical care) and those—including ours—that assert that meeting such needs is a private responsibility, undertaken as the extension of rights that are more directly political, including the right of ownership, of free speech, of elected governance, and so on.

Property rights are not simply fundamental to capitalistic democracy; they are a means by which such democracies define the nature of citizenship—the scope and setting for participation. Being American entails the possibility of ownership of a piece of America. Indeed, this was the prospect that lured – and continues to lure - unlanded millions to cross the oceans and deserts to get here. The siren call of the new world was the possibility of sharing in this dream of permanence, to begin a chain of successive inheritings that conferred a kind of immortality on those who settled here.

A commonplace of American historiography is the frontier thesis, which proposes that a deep epistemological break occurred in America when we had conquered our vast, unoccupied frontier. It was the presence of the frontier that fueled America's dynamic of possibility, and the "conquest" of the frontier implied that territory had been removed from the state of nature and "acquired" by rational actors in a rational society.

The seemingly endless American frontier sustained the Jeffersonian ideal by infinitely replenishing the national bank of land, defeating the idea of price, if only at the expanding edge and with its reserves of unappropriated property. As in Eden, where every need was available in abundance, there was no need for buying and selling: The land was simply there for the taking. Although this involved displacing (and slaughtering) the native Americans already living on it, the indigenous dwellers had no concept of property and were thus easily flummoxed by the new "enlightened" mentality of division and exchange.

No project is more emblematic of the mental and physical conquest of the frontier than the imposition of the mile-square Jeffersonian grid. The Jeffersonian grid was not simply a means of rendering territory measurable, hence rational, it was a configuration of the continent in logical increments of property, like the platting of a city into blocks. The Jeffersonian model further proposed that each square in the grid should support a citizen and his family. Implied were both an idea about self-sufficiency and a complementary idea about equality.

The idea that the organization of space is a conduit to the organization of mind was not exactly fresh to the eighteenth century, but rationalism put the connection on a more deliberate footing. Just as the gridded continent was understood as a means for creating a rational nation, so a debate immediately arose about a comparably rational architecture. Whether in the proliferation of utopian communities, the celebration of classical architecture as the wellspring of democracy, the repeated reproduction of the white-painted New England town with its church and green, or the fierce debate about correct form for prisons and asylums, early America was preoccupied with the value of architectural arrangements in the production of both happiness and reason.

In practice, however, attaining the Jeffersonian ideal was not so simple. Burgeoning cities with their free-form speculation in land, the rise of industrialization and the landless workers required to support it, the press of poor immigrants, and the slave economy all gave rise to numerous and unsustainable contradictions within the ambit of the idea of America and her special democracy. Yet despite the rapidly growing inequality of access to it, the dream of property endured. The grail of home ownership distinguishes us still in both the fact and the breach.

But the American idea of the benevolence of the market was not the only theoretical game in town. As the worker rapidly became the prototypical modern subject, displacing peasants, serfs, and farmers, the issue of property was reformulated. The new idea – derived from the efflorescence of various socialist and reformismist movements - was that one's rights extended beyond the right of ownership to the right to shelter. Faced with the immense stock of miserable housing that characterized the nineteenth century in both America and Europe, reformers co-opted the language of rights to argue that there were certain minimum housing standards to which all humans were entitled. These rights were based not only on an idea of fairness and on repulsion at the squalor of the industrial city but also on a "scientific", biological reading of the body politic.

The contemporary ethical, environmental, and social situation demands a new idea about both the quality and mix of housing. The single–family home, in particular, needs to be rigorously reexamined both to satisfy the needs of its dwellers and to be integrated into a more sustainable system of settlement.

By the middle of the nineteenth century, urban crowding was clearly understood as conducive to diseases, both of the body and the soul. Reformers, however, were caught in a middle territory. It was nobody's idea that the poor simply be given good housing. Rather, reformers sought to ensure that the housing that was provided for the poor offer some minimum standard of space, light, and sanitation, both for their own benefit and as a protection against the democracy of the epidemic, a threat to rich and poor alike. This idea of minimum standards was born of practicality, of the idea that poverty should not be rewarded, and—ultimately—on a new idea of equality that grew from the rise to consciousness of the working class.

The idea of the minimum was therefore rather rich. It was scientific in its efficiency, in the idea of an elegant coincidence between form and function. There was surely something Yankee in this, both in its mechanic character and in its disdain for excess. Moreover, the idea of the minimum was a constitutionally appropriate medium for the discussion of rights. Rights may be understood as a series of thresholds below which a particular right can no longer be said to exist. The task of articulating these thresholds against the background of the need for the massive creation of new housing became a debate of great liveliness, and ultimately gave rise to the formulation of the idea of the *existenzminimum*, the fundamental increment of shelter and an emblem of egalitarian architecture.

But one person's minimum existence is another's prison. The confluence of the disciplinary with the guarantee of a life space occurred early on, as the provision of housing came to be understood as both a boon to the ill-housed and as a means of keeping restive workers in line. Doing the least could be understood both as the definition of an entitlement and as the description of the very lowest degree of responsibility of the rich to the poor. Many of these considerations were subterranean: Two discourses described a single phenomenon, and shifting between them was a useful occlusion of actual feelings and intentions. The workers' housing of European modernism and the public housing of American reformism shared many formal characteristics but were far less aligned in intentions.

Which brings us close to the present. During the New Deal, the Federal Housing Administration established minimum standards for public-housing design, a native asymptote defining the putative line across which the spatially substandard could be understood. Compaction was embodied both in terms of the economies of construction but also in those of the ethics of entitlement and the virtues of living in a "ship-shape" environment, that is, one designed with scientific efficiency. Indeed, ocean liners were the great modernist prototype of mass-dwelling construction. Ships were unsentimental and hence rational, appropriately huge, very beautiful (in the *neue sachlichkeit* sense), and able to deploy elaborate class relations with great precision.

If the idea of the minimum suffused the provision of public housing, it also entered the discourse of private construction, the more mainstream branch of the American dream. Indeed, this bifurcation is a leading characteristic of the great period of American homebuilding that followed the Second World War. This was the era both of large-scale public-housing construction and of the growth of the suburbs, the result of the infusion of federal dollars into the housing market and into the infrastructure that defined where that market was to flourish.

The coincidence of cheap FHA loans for veterans, massive construction of highways, and a variety of other direct and indirect subsidies unleashed the sprawl that has now become the dominant form of American settlement. The mechanism of minima behind federal loans led directly to Levittown, the physical embodiment of the rigorously prescribed suburban ideal. Small houses on individual lots, redlined against integration, remade the ideal of the private house for the age of mass consumption and the culture of the car. Here, at last, were houses built according to assembly-line techniques that promised to revolutionize the provision of shelter by making it affordable by all—the dwelling as Model T.

The market has now segmented dramatically. Levittown represents an apotheosis of the idea of the melting pot, of the notion that the American dream entails a surrender of individual and cultural differences in order to share in a common enterprise and a universalized condition. The persistence of the idea of home ownership represents both the tenacity of this American model of democracy and happiness and a transmutation of the idea of difference into a set of stylistic tics and inflections and, of course, into the markers of wealth. This has led to its omega point, the current McMansion syndrome—bloated houses with three-car garages, staggering rates of resource consumption, grouped in fortified enclaves.

A current TV ad for a major real estate company features a car cruising down a long street lined with identical looking houses. In voice-over we hear a real estate agent trying to persuade his marks—who insist that they do not want to live in a ranch house—that this ranch house is actually Tudor and the next one Colonial—the kind of house they are actually looking for. The customers are unimpressed and likely to respond to the advertiser's claim that – unlike the agency mocked in the ad - it never shows a house that a potential buyer does not want to see.

The advertisement connects with a very general democratic ideal, that of choice. The perversion of this ideal by the mechanism of the market yields a thousand brands of cereal, inventory masquerading as choice. While it may be possible to distinguish among them via the infantile systems of taste they oblige, the constant is their lack of nutrition and staggering, addictive amounts of sugar. The housing market offers a similarly constrained product line, abundantly inflected to create apparent difference within the context of the single-family house. But this is not the choice we need, nor is its content the standard.

The contemporary ethical, environmental, and social situation demands a new idea about both the quality and mix of housing. The single-family home, in particular, needs to be rigorously reexamined both to satisfy the needs of its dwellers and to be integrated into a more sustainable system of settlement. In terms of energy, conservation, social life, and health, sprawl is a disaster. Dependent on automobiles, demanding disproportionate infrastructure investment, rapacious in its consumption of land, and a crucial origin point for our obesity and diabetes epidemics (ironic that hugeness now symbolizes mobility), the suburban model demands reform as a matter of both fairness and survival.

In this transformation, our evolving notion of the house must respect sustainable practices—lightening its lie on the land—and accommodate our social and individual differences. To follow through on this may require the dislodging of the single-family house from the top of the hierarchy of housing construction. It will also require new forms of collective responsibility, a post-NIMBY consciousness in which private interest extends into the public realm rather than simply ceasing at the edge of the sidewalk.

This again begs the question of the minimum. A reformed version of the minimum will use minimum energy, have a minimum ecological footprint, occupy a minimum territory. This does not necessarily imply that our per capita consumption of architectural space need shrink. Rather, it means that our share of such space must be calculated globally, in terms of the larger space of production and consumption, of the growing scarcity of planetary resources, and of our duty to share with those struggling for the minimum necessities of survival.

MS

According to the recent publication, The State of the Nation's Housing, by the Joint Center for Housing Studies of Harvard University, the demographics of those who can afford decent housing in this country has been on a downhill track since 1975. While the current low-interest rates and median incomes have made for the strongest year for housing on record, "a staggering three in ten U.S. households have housing affordability problems." The report continues, "Affordability remains America's most widespread housing challenge. The shortage of affordable housing directly affects the quality of life for the millions who eke out their housing payments every month, sacrifice the purchase of other essentials, commute long distances to work, and/or suffer overcrowded or unsafe conditions." Although the Triad region of North Carolina is a very affordable place to reside, housing problems do not escape this region either. For example, according to a recent report from the Brookings Institute, one-third of the Greensboro/Winston-Salem area residents cannot afford a one-bedroom apartment and 41 percent cannot afford a two-bedroom apartment. The average hourly wage needed to afford a one-bedroom apartment in 2003 was $8.87 in Greensboro, $9.40 in Charlotte, and $10.58 in Raleigh-versus the median wage for janitors of $7.30 in Greensboro, $7.47 in Charlotte, and $7.46 in Raleigh. Sales clerks earn a median wage in the same three cities of $7.78, $8.10, and $7.99, respectively. Without funding programs to help subsidize their mortgage, many residents would not qualify for affordable housing loans. In most areas, the problem of affordable housing is acute and a hotly contested issue.

David Hill, Matt Konar, Elizabeth Moore
Pearce Brinkley Cease & Lee
Raleigh, North Carolina

David J. Brown

Affordable housing is a noble cause with a bad history. As a people, Americans generously support the broad goal of helping our less fortunate acquire their own homes — but we don't want those homes to be constructed in our own neighborhoods. We hardly ever consider the type of materials that are incorporated into these types of buildings, much less how they are designed. The unfortunate reality is that most affordable housing looks exactly like what it is and adds to boundaries that quietly separate race, culture, and class.

But the social cost of bad design is only a part of its bad effect. Equally problematic is the pernicious effect of bad design on the environment. When taken as a whole, poorly designed and inefficient buildings are the worst polluters on the planet. They create massive amounts of waste and consume vast amounts of energy. According to the noted Columbian architect Simon Velez, "At one end of the chain is the misuse of non-renewable resources (mineral, energy, and others) by processing them into building materials and marketable products, and then assembling them into built structures; at the other, the rates of energy consumption which these kinds of buildings and infrastructure require for their use and maintenance."

Responsible design that respects the environment is variously called "environmentally friendly," "green," or "sustainable." The concept of sustainability can be traced back to President Theodore Roosevelt: "I recognize the right and duty of this generation to develop and use the natural resources of our land; but I do not recognize the right to waste them, or to rob, by wasteful use, the generations that come after us" (1910). But Roosevelt's vision has not always been America's reality. Our current method of supplying affordable housing is short-sighted and destructive. We focus on up-front costs, to the exclusion of long-term cost savings, health, and environmental benefits. We need to take a longer view: What does it take to maintain a house from start to finish? How does its construction and maintenance affect the environment? Can we develop a better model?

Developing a better model will require us to address sustainable and affordable housing design in dynamic and imaginative new ways. As Peter Buchanan, former deputy editor of *The Architectural Review* and curator of the exhibition *Ten Shades of Green* notes, "There is no such thing as a green architecture or a green aesthetic. Instead there are countless ways design can address and synthesize green issues. Green design is not merely a matter of add-ons or product specification. It involves more than insulation, low-emissivity glass, non-polluting paints, and water-conserving toilets. Rather, it influences the form of the whole building and is one of its major generators from the first moments of the design process. As a corollary, pursuing a green agenda is no constraint on creativity but instead a major stimulus toward an architecture that is innovative, significant, and relevant."

The unmistakable conclusion is this: We cannot continue to afford the design inefficiencies of our "affordable" housing. Our current behavior needs to change, and it's simply a matter of time until we will be forced as a society to do so. The good news is that we have already begun to address the problem. There are scores of resources available and countless individuals, programs, and businesses that are dedicated to helping us address our current needs in a way that will help conserve our natural resources for future generations. Community design organizations, university design-and-build programs, city initiatives, and even a few government programs are forging ahead.

Day by day, the public becomes more involved and better informed. The recent *Big and Green: Toward Sustainable Architecture in the 21st Century* exhibition at the National Building Museum in Washington, D.C., generated the second largest attendance in the museum's twenty-year history. Building supply centers have begun to offer some eco-friendly materials. If we demand them, governmental programs, tax and mortgage incentives will follow.

The Project
What might happen if well-designed homes for low- and moderate-income families began to flourish in established, even affluent neighborhoods? Could well-designed

Jim Fox, Leslie Ford, Marcus Bushong, Geoffrey Adams, Karen King
University of New Mexico, School of Architecture
Albuquerque, New Mexico

houses that use materials and methods carefully planned to be environmentally friendly be better not only for the planet but for the families that inhabit them? What would be the result if affordable, sustainable design became an important element in communities, city housing services, and manufactured housing organizations across the country? And how can a contemporary art museum aid in these endeavors? These are some of the questions raised by the Southeastern Center for Contemporary Art's HOME House Project.

The HOME House Project is concerned with the type of housing that is being offered in the affordable housing arena, the manner in which these houses are built, and the type of materials that are currently being used to build them.

A multi-year initiative, the HOME House Project is SECCA's effort to address the interrelated issues of design, affordability, and sustainability in housing. The HOME House Project features multiple components: a competition, exhibition, publication, educational programming, and a building phase—all of which are made possible by a large range of partnerships and collaborations with individuals, organizations, and communities.

The HOME House Project is a natural outgrowth of SECCA's long history of support for community-based projects. Best known, perhaps, is SECCA's nationally recognized *Artist and the Community* series, which began in 1993 as a residency program encouraging long-term collaboration between critically acclaimed artists, the museum, and community organizations. The *Artist and the Community* residencies promote the creation of new bodies of work that marry the personal interaction of artists and community residents with issues critical to the Piedmont region of North Carolina. Noted artists Fred Wilson, Maya Lin, Iñigo Manglano-Ovalle, Lesley Dill, and others have worked in concert with a variety of community groups, including schools, universities, libraries, churches, and social service agencies, many of which had no prior history of collaboration with SECCA.

Like the *Artist and the Community* series, the success of the HOME House Project depends on the museum's ability to foster close working relationships with a large

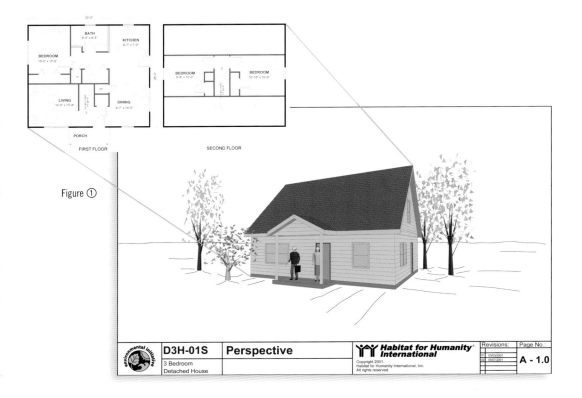

Figure ①

variety of collaborators. This nature of this collaboration means that the character of the HOME House Project will evolve as the contributions of individuals help define the shape of the initiative.

Initially, however, the HOME House Project is concerned with the type of housing that is being offered in the affordable housing arena, the manner in which these houses are built, and the type of materials that are currently being used to build them. Specifically, the project aims to provide inspired design for those individuals and families involved in the affordable housing market, a market that has historically seen very little innovation, let alone inspiration.

In the long run, the goal of the HOME House Project is to establish new standards of design, energy efficiency, environmental consciousness, and cost effectiveness that will constitute a new model for affordable housing in the United States. This model will showcase the most recent advances in sustainable design and foster new partnerships with people, organizations, and communities involved in the creative applications of affordable design across the United States.

The Competition and Exhibition

For the competition component of the HOME House Project, SECCA challenged artists and architects to propose new designs for affordable and sustainable single-family housing for low- and moderate-income families. Designs were informed by the building criteria and price parameters for typical three-and four-bedroom Habitat for Humanity houses, as specified by Habitat International in Americus, Georgia. SECCA chose one three-bedroom and one four-bedroom house design from the Habitat Planbook (figs. 1 and 2) and asked participants to use this information as a point of departure. Additionally, the design criteria focused on green and sustainable materials, technologies, and methods—areas that we feel housing, design, and construction must consider in the immediate future.

In addition to the general Habitat specifications, participants were given more specific parameters, which SECCA set according to the figures used by Winston-Salem's local Habitat chapter. The lot size in Winston-Salem is 140 by 60 feet, and a three-bedroom Habitat house sells for $65,000, a four-bedroom for $72,000. These figures do not account for site preparation and purchase (which can range up to $22,000), nor adjustments for the labor contributed by the volunteer labor force (even though Habitat does hire paid contractors), which averages about $15,000. Overall, roughly speaking, participants had to work within a budget of just over $100,000. (For other regions, that figure would be adjusted according to the local cost of living evaluation).

Habitat for Humanity House-Design Criteria
Habitat for Humanity's criteria for building simple and decent houses are outlined in its Affiliate Covenant.

The following points define the criteria affiliates should incorporate into their house designs:
1. The living space provided—excluding stairwells (except to a basement) and exterior storage—should not exceed:
   * 900 square feet for a two-bedroom house;
   * 1,050 square feet for a three-bedroom house;
   * 1,150 square feet for a four-bedroom house.
2. The basic house should have only one bathroom. This may be compartmentalized for increased usefulness, or additional baths may be added by the family as part of their budget (see #3).
3. Families should have an opportunity to affect the design of their houses as much as possible. A budget should be established with a predetermined limit (e.g., $1,000) to allow the family to personalize their home with such features as picture windows, fencing, half-bath, etc.
4. Each house should have a covered primary entrance.
5. When feasible, at least one entrance to the house should be accessible to persons who have difficulty with mobility.
6. All passage doors, including the bathroom door, should be three feet (3') wide. Halls should be at least three feet and four inches (3' 4") wide from frame to frame. (Note: if there is a door in the hallway, minimum width increases to three feet and seven inches (3' 7").) These standards allow for simple access for persons with disabilities and increase the cost only slightly. Further adaptations may be needed if a family member is disabled.
7. Homes should not have garages or carports.
Note: Although rehabilitation projects may provide a set of circumstances in which some of the above guidelines cannot be met, affiliates should maintain the intent and spirit of the guidelines when determining the specifics and extent of the proposed rehabilitation. Used with permission from Habitat International, Americus, Georgia

The combination of criteria we specified for the HOME House Project competition offered a way to engage low-and moderate-income families, communities, cultural, humanitarian, and, perhaps, commercial organizations in the advantages of sustainability, quality design, and workmanship.

Response to the HOME House Project's call for entries was overwhelming. From over 800 worldwide registrants, more than 440 individuals and teams from across the United States and six countries submitted designs. The designs were exhibited initially at SECCA from May 9 through July 6, 2003, and again from October 19 through April 3, 2004. Participants offered a range of design solutions—from the adventurous and visionary, whose construction techniques are several years away, to more traditional approaches that incorporate today's materials, and everything in between. Because the call for entries had not established a category distinction between novice and professional, the pool of entered designs inevitably showed a wide range of understanding and implementation of sustainable-design processes.

Some participants believed that creating a new housing model required them to rethink the entire process of designing and building a home. Others were satisfied to confine their efforts to exploring today's construction and financing options, available products, and technologies. The number and variety of designs entered demonstrate the interest of

Beth Blostein
Blostein/Overly Architects
Columbus, Ohio

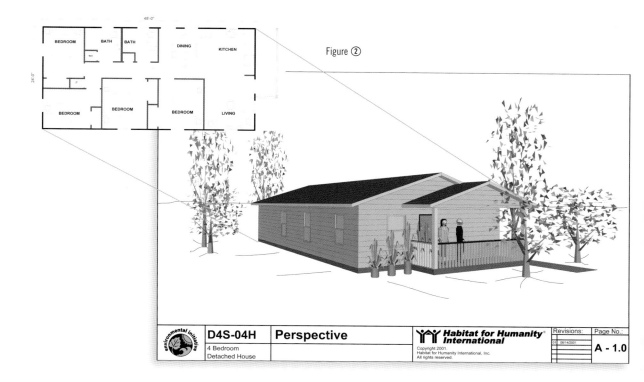

Figure ②

D4S-04H | Perspective | Habitat for Humanity International
4 Bedroom Detached House
Copyright 2001. Habitat for Humanity International, Inc. All rights reserved.
Revisions: 01 06/14/2001
Page No.: A - 1.0

architects in addressing pertinent social issues and prove that as technology changes, so does our ability to consider and actualize new solutions to housing problems.

SECCA enlisted the expertise of noted architects, educators, authors, designers, and builders Michael Sorkin, Ben Nicholson, and Steve Badanes to select twenty-five Proposals of Merit and award monetary prizes. The jury convened in early May 2003, and after much discussion, decided that due to the egalitarian nature of the project, the award money should be divided equally among the selected winners.

- Beth Blostein's *Gradient House* (left) proposed a polycarbonate panel skin over a greenhouse frame in which every passive and mechanical system has been rethought. Blostein uses a digitally fabricated central wall system made from recycled plastics to construct house ductwork, wiring runs, closets, and even appliances. The unit acts as a conduit between "an equipment space loft and a ground coil geothermal heating and cooling system unit installed under the house pad."
- S. Flavio Espinoza, formerly with William McDonough's office in Charlottesville, Virginia, produced a straight-ahead sustainable design that marries traditional "Southern" vernacular architecture with a modern stance. His butterfly roof is designed to capture rainwater for a variety of

purposes, including both heating and cooling the house. Wooden shutters on the south-facing walls of the house use a hanging track system that allows them to be manually operated. Simple and efficient.

- Mitchell Joachim, Lara Greden and Javier Arbona (Team H.E.D.), M.I.T. School of Architecture proposed a tree house whose living organic structure is formed by the systematic bending and controlled growth of live tree branches (known as pleaching). (Note: The construction phase for this unit is probably about seventy years.)
- Steven Raike, of Bear Creek, Pennsylvania, offered a three-story building perched atop an existing industrial building in a dense urban area (in a semi-parasitic, guest-host relationship) where one side of the structure sports a billboard that could help offset mortgage payments. In Raike's words, "This unit of habitation is essentially an adaptive re-use of vacant urban space."
- San Francisco's Peter Strzebniok and Matthias Troitszch opted for a variety of solutions to a central plan. According to the two, "The design is a modular pre-fabricated housing system that incorporates production principles from the automobile industry into architecture, providing flexible and affordable housing solutions for different income levels, site requirements, and owner preferences."
- Other designs incorporated the overabundance of reusable shipping containers recycled in a variety of ways, some more successful than others: green, living roofs and walls; roofs of varying shapes and slopes used for a variety of purposes; straw bale homes; variations derived from the study of the mobile and manufactured home culture, and interchangeable component houses.

Building phase

The second component of the HOME House Project is a multi-year building phase. SECCA will partner with builders, schools, financing organizations, and other organizations in the affordable housing infrastructure to construct a series of houses for low-and moderate-income families. We will begin the building phase in Winston-Salem, but our plan is for the HOME House Project to spread to other areas in North Carolina and expand to other states using the Winston-Salem model as a guide.

The Housing Partnership of Winston-Salem/Forsyth County, Inc. is the first organization to team with SECCA in the HOME House Project's building phase. The Housing Partnership is the local office of a national organization. It has over 300 building sites throughout the city of Winston-Salem. Executive Director Jane Milner intends to take the proceeds from the sale of the initial two HOME House Project houses to build four additional structures.

   To build the first structure, SECCA is also partnering with Forsyth Technical Community College's construction and engineering departments and the city of Winston-Salem. Forsyth Tech produced the working construction drawings for the first house and created thirteen three-dimensional computer animations from the award-winning HOME House Project entries. By insisting to construct the first house, Tech's students and faculty will develop skills that will help them build sustainable houses throughout their careers. The first design, a selection by award winner S. Flavio Espinoza will be constructed in the Holly Avenue neighborhood in Winston- Salem.

   Future building projects are already in the works. A second group, Sustainable Housing, LLC., headed by businessmen William Benton and Bud Baker, are working with the city in an effort to build six houses in the same neighborhood as the first unit.

John Nelson
College of Architecture, University
of North Carolina - Charlotte
Charlotte, North Carolina

When the house design was presented at the neighborhood association meeting, it was approved unanimously by the community residents. In addition, a second group, headed by businessmen William Benton and Bud Baker, are working with the city in an effort to build six houses in the same neighborhood as the first unit, an area near downtown that is the city's seventh district named to the National Register of Historic Places.

Building for the Future

With the HOME House Project, a contemporary art museum has provided a forum for artists, designers, and architects to address the range of issues surrounding affordable housing. The project aims to champion the work of individuals and organizations who have been actively engaged in these activities over time, and to encourage organizations in the affordable housing arena to incorporate high-quality design and sustainable policies into their infrastructures. Following our lead, many of the cultural organizations hosting the HOME House Project exhibition are collaborating with affordable housing groups, businesses, and architectural groups to bring the project to fruition in their particular city. In Baltimore, the Center for Visual Arts and Culture, University of Maryland, Baltimore County is teaming with the Community Design Center and the American Institute of Architects, Baltimore Chapter. The Neighborhood Housing Services of Asheville is teaming with the Asheville Art Museum, the Green Buildings Council, Asheville Buncombe Technical Community College and others to bring the show to the Public Works building in Downtown Asheville. These kinds of collaborative efforts rarely occur in the art world.

In closing, we wish to notify all affordable-housing organizations, manufactured and housing industries, builders, planners, city and government officials, policy makers, individuals, families, and communities: The HOME House Project is coming your way and has the potential to change the face of affordable housing in the United States, highlight recent advances in sustainable technology and products, and point to outdated policies that fuel the continuation of a geographical, social, and class-based housing prejudice in communities everywhere. None of us can accomplish this feat alone, but by working together and sharing our talent and resources, we can make a difference.

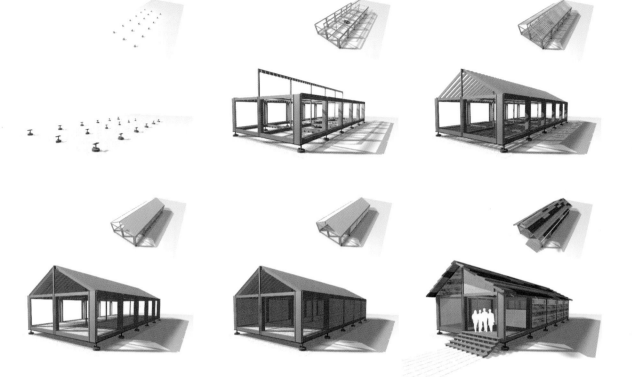

Joe Meppelink, Adam Janusz,
Onezieme Mouton, Wyatt Frantom
FrameWork
Houston, Texas

25 Awards of Merit

Selected by jurors

Steve Badanes
Ben Nicholson
Michael Sorkin

Jim Fox, Leslie Ford, Marcus
Bushong, Geoffrey Adams,
Karen King
*University of New Mexico,
School of Architecture and Planning
Albuquerque, New Mexico*

Beth Blostein
*Blostein/Overly Architects
Columbus, Ohio*

Zan Bross
Cambridge, Massachusetts

W.G. Clark, Azadeh Rashidi,
Joshua Stastny
*W.G. Clark Associates Architects
Charlottesville, Virginia*

Matias Creimer
Los Angeles, California

Adin L. Dunning, Wayne
Chevalier, Jeremy Fredricks
*bracket
Portland, Oregon*

S. Flavio Espinoza
Sag Harbor, New York

Jeff Alan Gard
San Francisco, California

Douglas Gauthier, Jeremy
Edmiston
*SYSTEMarchitects
New York, New York*

Daniela Fabricius
Brooklyn, New York

Mario Gentile, Andrew Hart,
Reed Crittenden
Brooklyn, New York

Keith Evan Green
*School of Architecture
Clemson University
Clemson, South Carolina*

Rado Ivanov
*Studio R22
Alexandria, Virginia*

Mitchell Joachim, Lara
Greden, Javier Arbona
*Team H.E.D.
MIT School of Architecture
Cambridge, Massachusetts*

Joseph Karadin
Forest Hills, New York

Kenneth Kim, Paula Rosales,
Wojtek Sosnowski
*MOREMAS
New York, New York*

Joe Meppelink, Adam Janusz,
Onezieme Mouton, Wyatt Frantom
*Framework
Houston, Texas*

Mark Nye
Lambertville, New Jersey

Drura Parrish
Los Angeles, California

Ronald Rael, Patricio del Real
Seneca, South Carolina

Steven Raike
Bear Creek, Pennsylvania

Studio 804
*Design Build Studio
University of Kansas
Lawrence, Kansas*

*aandacht loop/Morpurgo
Architects (ALMA)
Ho-Ho-Kus, New Jersey*

Peter Strzebniok/Matthias
Troitzsch
*NOTTOSCALE
San Francisco, California*

Tricia Stuth, Ted Shelton
Cambridge, England

Dog Trot House

**Jim Fox, Leslie Ford, Marcus Bushong,
Geoffrey Adams, Karen King**
*University of New Mexico, School of Architecture and Planning
Albuquerque, New Mexico*

Dog Trot Revisited

Inspired by the dog trot house type, this house consists of two affordable 40' x 8' x 8.5' shipping containers, separated by a central space. The North container holds the kitchen and appliances (including washer, dryer, water heater), pantry/outdoor storage (bicycles, lawn mower, tools), and the bathroom. The South container is the bedroom wing. Front and back glass doors provide ventilation and connect the inside with the outside veranda. Instead of bringing the outside in, the house opens up to nature and neighbors, becoming an outdoor room that capitalizes on the moderate weather in Winston-Salem.

Building Process

Two shipping containers arrive at the site with all insulation and utility service components installed. Containers and simple wood flat decks are placed on concrete piers. Bathrooms, closets and bedrooms can be finished out on site. A simple flat roof is built and installed on-site.

Divergence from Excess

Nearly 95% of all imported goods coming into the United States arrive in some type of shipping container. Due to the current and increasing U.S. trade deficit, there is an overabundance of these durable containers available for shipping and alternative use. In addition, it is also estimated that the number of containers arriving in the U.S. annually will double in the next 20 years.

Materials

Container and counter finishes are customized to homeowner's specifications. Framing, floor, ceiling, movable built-in platform beds, under-bed storage drawers/step, and closets are made with engineered lumber. Bath walls, door and kitchen pantry are built of recycled corrugated fiberglass roofing. South facing bedrooms open to utilize passive solar energy. Sliding entry doors are built with recycled glass doors. Hollow light-weight interior doors pivot and slide on vertical columns to turn corners and tuck away flush with walls. Insulation is wool batt (made from recycled denim) or paper pulp insulation. A workshop, additional storage or a mother-in-law suite can later be added to the home by installing an 8' x 20' container to the existing structure. Bath and kitchen counters would be constructed with homeowner's choice of poured sealed concrete, Icestone (made from local recycled glass from the nearby bottling plant) or tile.

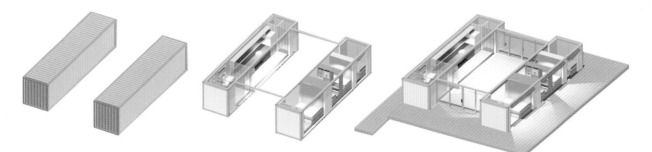

Landscaping

Landscaping could be kept natural and minimal or be used to create an architecture of green that extends the space aesthetically into the open air area. The house would come with a garden budget to include optional set-up of a raised vegetable, cutting or herb garden.

Flexibility and Comfort

Flexible space, universally designed, adapts to different stages of family life and different privacy and/or entertaining situations. Low maintenance design is easy to keep clean, and ready to move in (i.e.: furniture built-ins). The space forms a retreat to feel safe and enjoy nature. And, the rugged structure and materials withstand children and pets.

WEST   NORTH

Gradient House

Beth Blostein

Blostein/Overly Architects
Columbus, Ohio

This 3 bedroom **GRADIENT HOUSE** utilizes a prefabricated 22'x33' green-house frame laminated with translucent polycarbonate panels that adequately resist snow, wind, and impact loads.

Shade cloth is used to provide protection from the sun in summer as well as allow privacy without compromising the natural lighting. The configuration of the system changes based both on the house's sun orientation and on owner privacy considerations.

A molded system wall embeds many amenities of the home into one unit including plumbing and stubouts, ventilation ducts, electrical runs, closets and other built-in cabinetry-- even sinks! It is molded in a shop from recycled plastic with a fiberglass additive, a material used widely today in the production of synthetic structural lumber. This material is quite strong and will support conventional construction as well as home equipment such as the refrigerator, stackable washer/dryer, and television. The return on the system wall is twofold: one, square footage, allowing the GRADIENT HOUSE's three bedroom version to have large family spaces, including a second floor playroom that could double as an office or be modified to become an additional bedroom; and two, a reduction of skilled labor at the site given that most of this work arrives prefabricated as a part of the wall.

Mechanically, the system wall becomes a conduit between an equipment space loft and a ground coil geothermal heating and cooling system, which is installed under the house pad.

POLYCARBONATE PANELS
super strong, translucent twinwall panel can easily sustain snow and wind loading. Panels arrive at site filled with Aerogel, a translucent material that is highly insulating.

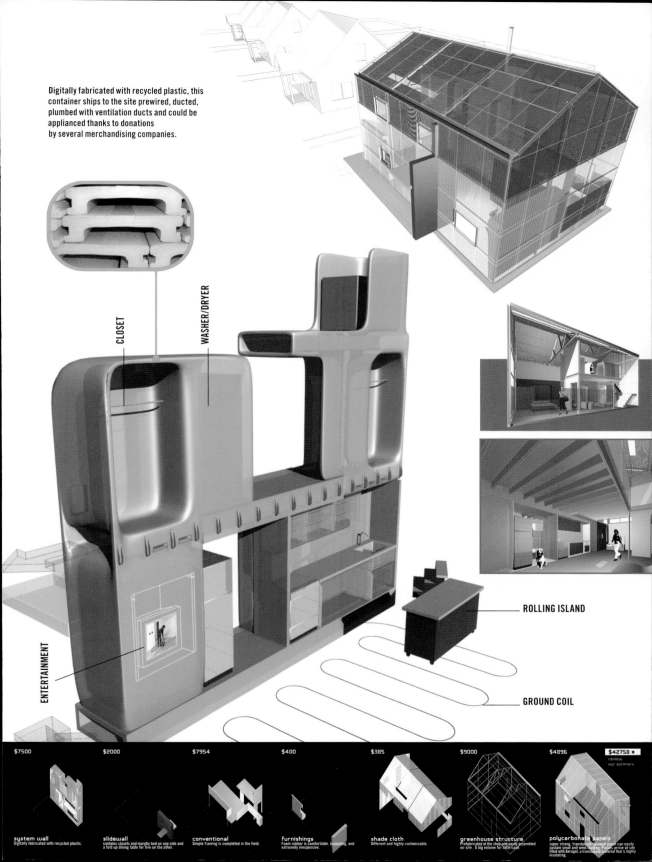

Digitally fabricated with recycled plastic, this container ships to the site prewired, ducted, plumbed with ventilation ducts and could be applianced thanks to donations by several merchandising companies.

CLOSET

WASHER/DRYER

ENTERTAINMENT

ROLLING ISLAND

GROUND COIL

$7500	$2000	$7954	$400	$385	$9000	$4896	**$42758 ∗**
							review our estimate

system wall
Digitally fabricated with recycled plastic.

slidewall
contains closets and murphy bed on one side and a fold up dining table for live on the other.

conventional
Simple framing is completed in the field.

furnishings
Foam rubber is comfortable, insulating, and extremely inexpensive.

shade cloth
Different and highly customizable.

greenhouse structure
Prefabricated at the shop and easily assembled on-site. A big volume for little cash.

polycarbonate panels
super strong, translucent fanwall panel can easily sustain snow and wind loading. Panels arrive at site filled with Aerogel, a translucent material that is highly insulating.

Rural South / Modern Living

Zan Bross

Cambridge, Massachusetts

2nd Floor Plan

1st Floor Plan

DESIGN SUMMARY

Based on the aesthetic of vernacular architecture in the rural south, this design works conventional materials and simple forms into a home that addresses the needs of modern living. Through the open floor plan, the kitchen and living room work in tandem to provide a social gathering place for family and friends. The bathroom and master bedroom are both on the first floor. Designed to accommodate anyone with accessibility needs, these two spaces both have rolling pocket doors. There are two bedrooms upstairs with a study alcove between the two. This study alcove, designed for a computer workstation, could be built as a dormer and accommodate a second bath instead. Having the long dimension of the home facing south is advantageous for passive solar heating during the winter while sun shades block out the steep rays during the summer months. The full front porch at the entry, not uncommon to homes in this region, provides a sheltered entrance into the home. Semi-transparent polycarbonate roofing material on the porch roof allows morning sun to penetrate into the kitchen. A ramp for accessibility could easily be added parallel to the stairs if necessary.

CONSTRUCTION AND MATERIALS

The simplicity of the form enables this project to be built easily with limited-skilled labor. Engineered floor joists can clear span the first and second floor framing while 2"x8" dimensional lumber will frame the roof rafters. The front porch is made of non-CCA dimensional lumber and the patio can be made of either reclaimed concrete pavers or a grass paver system. Recycled content OSB sheathing with a housewrap air infiltration barrier will cover the 2"x6" framed walls. All walls will be insulated with non-toxic wet blown wall insulation. The exterior siding will be a combination of 2 styles of corrugated metal as suggested by the renderings. The roof will be a standing seam painted steel roof for its durability and aesthetic. It will also be 1 less asphalt roof to dump into a land fill in the future. Double-glazed low-E vinyl-clad wood windows and skylights will provide ample natural light for all the living spaces and discourage the use of electrical lighting during the day. The interior walls will be finished with recycled-content gypsum wall board and painted in light colors to reflect natural light. The flooring will be either bamboo or salvaged hardwood in all spaces except the ceramic-tiled bathroom. To help aid in water conservation, the on-demand electronic ignition gas hot-water heater will be located in the bathroom linen closet, close to all the plumbing fixtures. The stackable washer and electronic ignition gas dryer will be in a utility closet in the kitchen.

View from the south

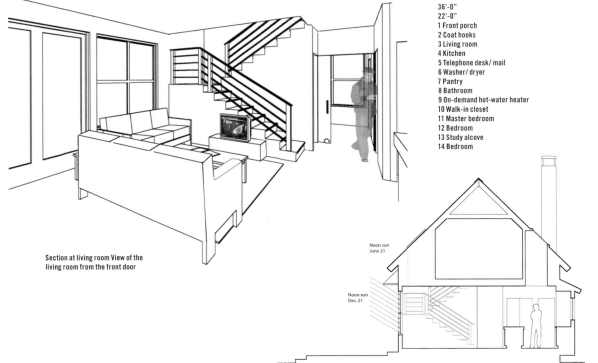

Section at living room View of the
living room from the front door

36'-0"
22'-0"
1 Front porch
2 Coat hooks
3 Living room
4 Kitchen
5 Telephone desk/ mail
6 Washer/ dryer
7 Pantry
8 Bathroom
9 On-demand hot-water heater
10 Walk-in closet
11 Master bedroom
12 Bedroom
13 Study alcove
14 Bedroom

Noon sun
June 21

Noon sun
Dec. 21

winners

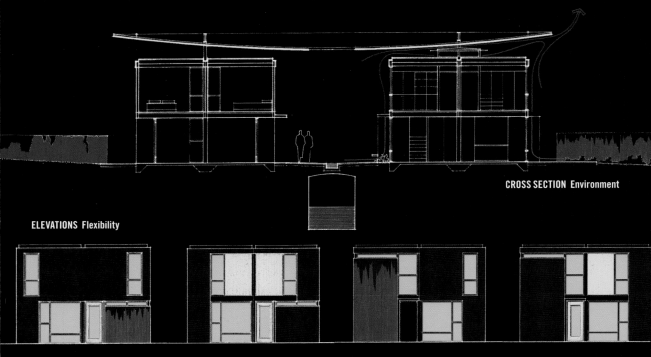

CROSS SECTION Environment

ELEVATIONS Flexibility

Collective Dwelling

W.G. Clark, Azadeh Rashidi,
Joshua Stastny

W.G. Clark Associates Architects
Charlottesville, Virginia

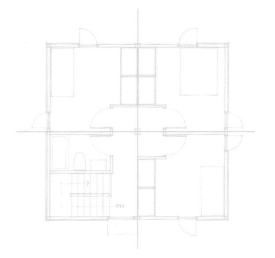

Density

The single family detached dwelling supports and extends suburban sprawl. By placing dwellings in a denser collective form, land is conserved while a community is formed which may benefit from the mutual economies of shared resources, beginning with the land itself. The form of the collective can vary to suit different sites and road adjacencies. The variable units may be either spaced or abutted, with all rooms having windows.

Sustainability + Environment

The over arching principle of sustainability is the preservation of the land. Additionally, the houses share an energy canopy and a infrastructural base. The suspended fabric canopy collects rain water for community use; provides shade; provides a solar surface for adhesive photovoltaic strips; and creates an enhanced natural ventilation for the houses. The concrete plinth that is both a pedestrian street and a foundation slab for the houses contains channels for utilities and cisterns for non-potable water use. Energy consumption shall be reduced further within the individual units through responsible choices, such as the use of geothermal systems.

Community

The collective form creates a community through density and the shared interest in the preservation of natural resources. Human interaction is encouraged along the internal street, the community court, and gardens. The community is to overcome the monolithic social condition of suburbia that only addresses families by including units for singles and the elderly, thereby creating diversity.

Modularity + Flexibility

The design of the houses is based on a modular system which incorporates wide variations and allows for subsequent additions and modifications. The benefits of a modular system of construction in terms of efficiency and cost effectiveness are obvious. However, the challenge is for the system to allow for individuality. Beyond the permutative aspects of the module related to the number of bedrooms, there is a secondary "kit of parts" with which individual residents may personalize their homes. This is allowed for through cladding and fenestration choices, as well as additive "landscapes". The module allows for the units to be built by the community, which we feel outweighs the economics of prefab.

CLADDING: Kit of parts

CORRUGATED METAL   CEMENT BOARD   HORIZONTAL WOOD SIDING   PLANTED WALLS   VERTICAL WOOD SIDING

LONGITUDINAL SECTION Environment

View of internal street

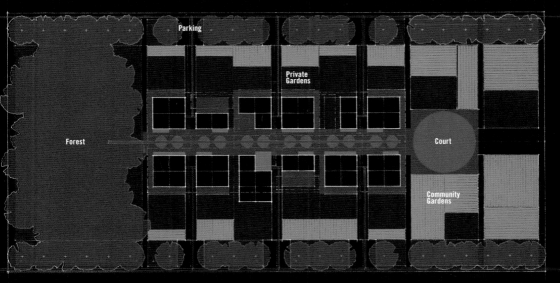

Parking

Private
Gardens

Forest

Court

Community
Gardens

SITE PLAN Sustainable Community

Production
Modern zoning attitudes discourage the productive landscape in favor of lawns.
This project envisions the reintegration of cultivation with the dwelling and
allows for the coexistence of wilderness, cultivation, and urbanity.

Dockable Dwelling

Matias Creimer
Los Angeles, California

This project proposes to finally inject the notion of efficiency into the design and construction of affordable houses, in order to allow a low, fixed budget to pay for more. It is a factory-assembled modular system that "couples" the components of a house as easily as the middle cars of a train.

Visiting a construction site reveals both the beauty of hands on craftsmanship and its inefficiency. Bricks, stones, mortar, wood joists, posts, tiles, pipes, nails, they all represent areas where a big portion of a small budget is allocated. Given the low-tech nature of these trades, the latest technological revolution is of little or no help.

As technology fueled, assembly-lined robotics and qualified labor bring down the price of highly sophisticated, exquisitely designed items [such as phones, computers, cars] the construction of houses is still at the mercy of the weather. This was unavoidable in the past for any building, and it is still unavoidable now for buildings over a certain size. The critical size that obstructs the shipment of high-tech factory assembled buildings, or building modules, is set by the infrastructure needed to transport them. But houses are below that critical size. This means that the obstacle that keeps affordable house design and production from joining all the other industries in benefiting from the developments brought about by the technological revolution is not of a physical nature.

Borrowing NASA's approach to "space station modular docking", where minimizing space walking time is critical, this project proposes a collection of modules to be fully built in factory with almost no on-site assembly required: level up a portion of the site, plug the modules together and leave.

In order to promote diversity and competition this project proposes the adoption of a single "universal docking port" system that would ensure compatibility among different modules manufactured and designed by different companies. By the time they leave the factory, all modules should be fully insulated, all finishes applied, and all ducts, wires and pipes should be fully installed and converging to specific points on the faces of the universal docking ports.

Regarding the energy efficiency of these houses, with the use of technology and in-factory assembly it should be possible to merge the skinning of the modules with the installation of Solar energy collecting systems, resulting in a single photovoltaic-insulating membrane.

3 Bedroom unit / 1300 sf

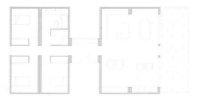

4 Bedroom unit / 1600 sf

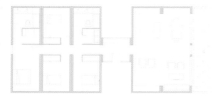

Delivery of unit

The modularity and transportability of these houses should encourage homeowners with different plans for their site, to sell their used modules instead of destroying them. By the end of their life cycle, and given the expected similarities with the products of the automotive production industry, it should be possible for these modules to be absorbed by the automotive recycling industry.

DIGITAL
ELECTRICAL
HVAC RETURN
PLUMBING
SOLAR
ELECTRICAL
PLUMBING
HVAC SUPPLY
MISCALLANEOUS
SEWAGE

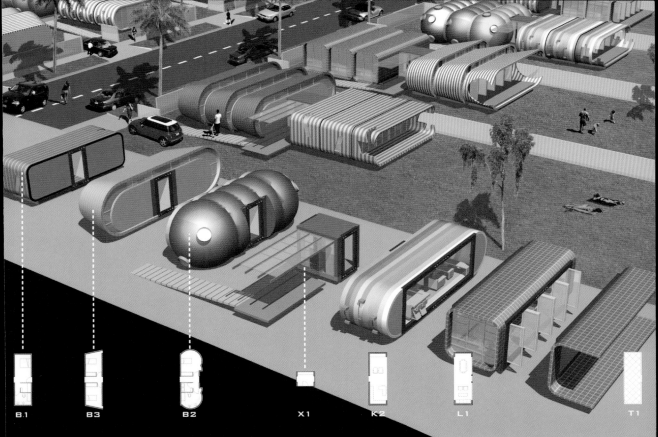

B.1   B3   B2   X1   K2   L1   T1

U.03 House

**Adin L. Dunning, Wayne Chevalier,
Jeremy Fredricks**

*bracket
Portland, Oregon*

The u.03 house reinterprets the standard habitat design, utilizing what has been the traditional house program. This solution is designed to incorporate common construction techniques, modular components, an efficient and compact design, and well thought out and easy to build and operate systems, simultaneously providing a comfortable and inspiring living space sensitive to its environment.

In order to reduce first-costs, the home is designed to utilize as many modular components and to capitalize on unskilled labor as the 'assemblers', while more complicated tasks can occur off-site. These pre-fabricated components allow for the economy of scale when considering they can be manufactured for many homes at once. This 'kit', then, can be shipped to the site via a single container, minimizing delivery costs. In addition, this modularity allows for ease of plan customization. The design options for the family are truly endless.

Central to the design is a structural and systems 'spine', which allows for the shortest and straightest run of plumbing and conduit, while simultaneously providing structural support. Systems are simple to build and operate, given the straight-forward design.

The u.03 home design capitalizes on the finishes and character of the materials used in the structure. Rather than spending money and natural resources to wrap everything with gypsum, the design is honest in its exposure of materials. Steel, plywood, concrete, and masonry are all strategically used throughout the home. There are also many opportunities to adapt the home's finishes to a particular region or a families preference. For instance, the structural spine wall may be rammed-earth or hay bale, as climate and client allow.

With political, economic, and social conditions as they are in today's world, responsible design in terms of first costs, reliance on tradition fossil fuels, and the environmental 'footprint' our buildings leave must be minimized. Good design should not be an exclusive right of the wealthy or environmentally irresponsible

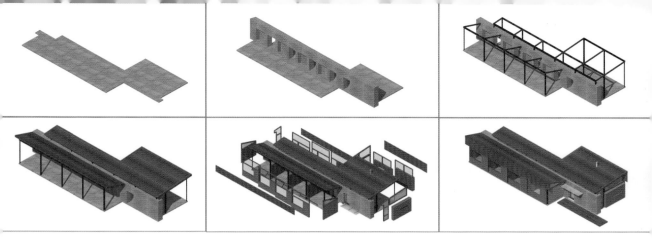

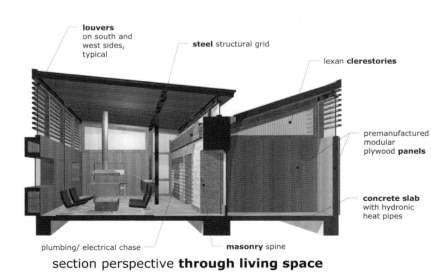

louvers
on south and
west sides,
typical

steel structural grid

lexan clerestories

premanufactured
modular
plywood panels

concrete slab
with hydronic
heat pipes

plumbing/ electrical chase

masonry spine

section perspective through living space

Suburban Loft

S. Flavio Espinoza
Sag Harbor, New York

First Floor Plan

Second Floor Plan

Traditional Poetics with Contemporary Pragmatics

This investigation began as a simple design assignment: "provide residents of low and moderate-income housing with inspired living space usually reserved for the more affluent. Our overall aim is to establish a new national housing model in terms of design, energy efficiency, environmental consciousness, sustainability, and cost effectiveness [affordability] that will be used throughout the state of North Carolina and perhaps the rest of the country."

As the investigation evolved the ideas of "affordability" and "sustainability" were brought into question, and found to be connected. Three key questions drove the design process. What is affordability? What is sustainability? What do these ideas mean to low and moderate-income families? The solution brings together the best aspects of suburban and urban living space, while challenging the traditional notions of affordability and sustainability.

The design drew its inspiration from three main precedents. The first was the detached single-family house. Archetypal examples such as porch, pitched roof, shutters, double hung windows, and rain screens were drawn from the single family home. The integration is a reinterpretation of the housing traditions of the past guided by ecological effective principles. The shutters are not appliqué. They work on a track system that allows the homeowner to manage the light penetration through out the year. The double hung windows operability is key to the cross-ventilation strategy. The rain screen is designed to also act as a thermal blanket helping to insulate the exterior wall. The pitched roof is reversed from the traditional gable to a "butterfly" which drains into a cistern for domestic non-potable water use. The roofs angle is also optimized for solar hot water integration. Every aspect of the design was scrutinized for its aesthetic, ecological effectiveness and affordability.

What is affordability? What this means to a low or moderate income family is that the initial affordability of a $70,000 subsidized loan over 30 years is irrelevant if the energy costs of the house surpass the income growth of the household. If the home is not designed to its full ecological potential, in order to hedge against the growing energy crisis, we may put these families in a worse economic position then they were in.

What is sustainability? To a low-income family this arguably means sustaining the family. This could be as simple as putting food on the table.

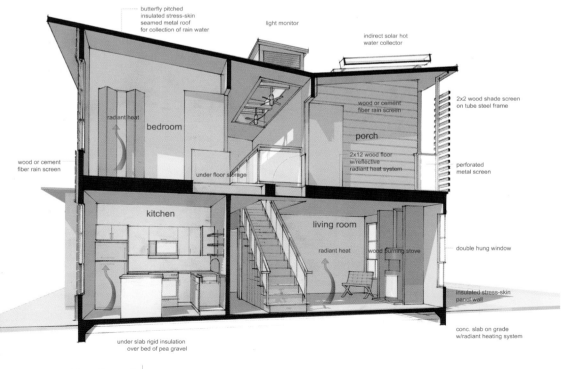

Section 1 | along EW axis

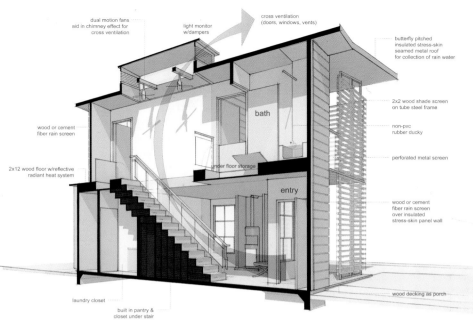

dual motion fans
aid in chimney effect for
cross ventilation

light monitor
w/dampers

cross ventilation
(doors, windows, vents)

butterfly pitched
insulated stress-skin
seamed metal roof
for collection of rain water

bath

2x2 wood shade screen
on tube steel frame

non-pvc
rubber ducky

perforated metal screen

under floor storage

wood or cement
fiber rain screen

entry

wood or cement
fiber rain screen
over insulated
stress-skin panel wall

2x12 wood floor w/reflective
radiant heat system

wood decking as porch

laundry closet

built in pantry &
closet under stair

gutter for rain water
collection

insulated stress-skin
w/seamed metal roof

sliding wood shutter
on tube steel frame

downspout from
butterfly roof

wood or cement
fiber rain screen

insulated stress-skin
w/seamed metal roof

cistern to collect
rain water for
non potable use

cement fiber panel
over insulated
stress-skin wall

double hung window

North West Corner view looking SE

Section 2 along NS axis

The second and third precedents
were the loft and the Japanese
Tatami house, which guided
the interior composition. These
archetypes were chosen due to
limited area requirements. These
designs are examples of how
minimal space can be utilized to its
maximum potential.

As fossil fuel prices rise and mean incomes
fall, sustainable technology is less a luxury
and more a necessity. With new growth
inevitable we must ask ourselves if we can
afford to continue with housing strategies
which ignore long term benefits for the
home owner; both economically and
environmentally. This project took these
ideas and rather than creating solutions,
it asked the observer questions. What is
affordability? What is sustainability? What
does this mean to the low-income family?

butterfly pitched
insulated stress-skin
seamed metal roof
for collection of rain water

chimney

sliding wood shutter
on tube steel frame

wood or cement
fiber rain screen

insulated stress-skin
w/seamed metal roof

insulated stress-skin
w/seamed metal roof

cement fiber panel
over insulated
stress-skin wall

sliding wood shutter
on tube steel frame

double hung windows

wood or cement
fiber rain screen

2x2 wood shade screen
on tube steel frame

South East Corner view looking NW

5. The combination of existing energy efficient technology in a
new way hopes to exponentially expand the energy savings to
the home owner.

4. The radiant floor system is connected to a second instant hot
water heater which replaces the traditional boiler which also
heats the water even when there is no direct demand.

3. Domestic hot water is brought in through a similar heat
exchange coil through the radiant floor tank. This increases
the temperature of the source water which in turn reduces the
energy needed to heat the water to the desired temperature.
When water is needed an instant hot water system heats the
water to the desired temperature on demand. This eliminates
the need for a traditional hot water tank which expends energy
keeping the water hot even when no hot water is needed.

There is also a bypass in case of leakage which diverts the
source water directly to the instant hot water heater.

2. A heat exchange coil transfers the heat from the solar pipes
to the radiant floor water tank. This reduces the energy needed
to heat the water for the floor system.

1. Solar collectors on the roof are filled with ethylene glycol
(antifreeze). The heat collected from them is transferee to a
water tank via pipes in the wall.

Single Family Home

Jeff Alan Gard
San Francisco, California

The habitat team arrives to a site shaded by graceful canopies. The canopies are factory built, waterproofed, insulated, delivered and installed. Protected from rain and shaded from the sun, the task of tilting up the non-bearing walls begins.

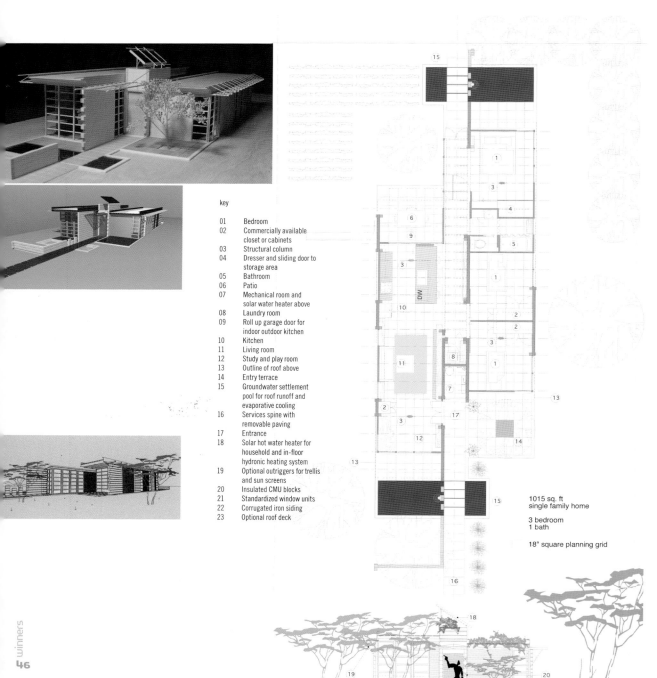

key

01 Bedroom
02 Commercially available closet or cabinets
03 Structural column
04 Dresser and sliding door to storage area
05 Bathroom
06 Patio
07 Mechanical room and solar water heater above
08 Laundry room
09 Roll up garage door for indoor outdoor kitchen
10 Kitchen
11 Living room
12 Study and play room
13 Outline of roof above
14 Entry terrace
15 Groundwater settlement pool for roof runoff and evaporative cooling
16 Services spine with removable paving
17 Entrance
18 Solar hot water heater for household and in-floor hydronic heating system
19 Optional outriggers for trellis and sun screens
20 Insulated CMU blocks
21 Standardized window units
22 Corrugated iron siding
23 Optional roof deck

1015 sq. ft
single family home

3 bedroom
1 bath

18" square planning grid

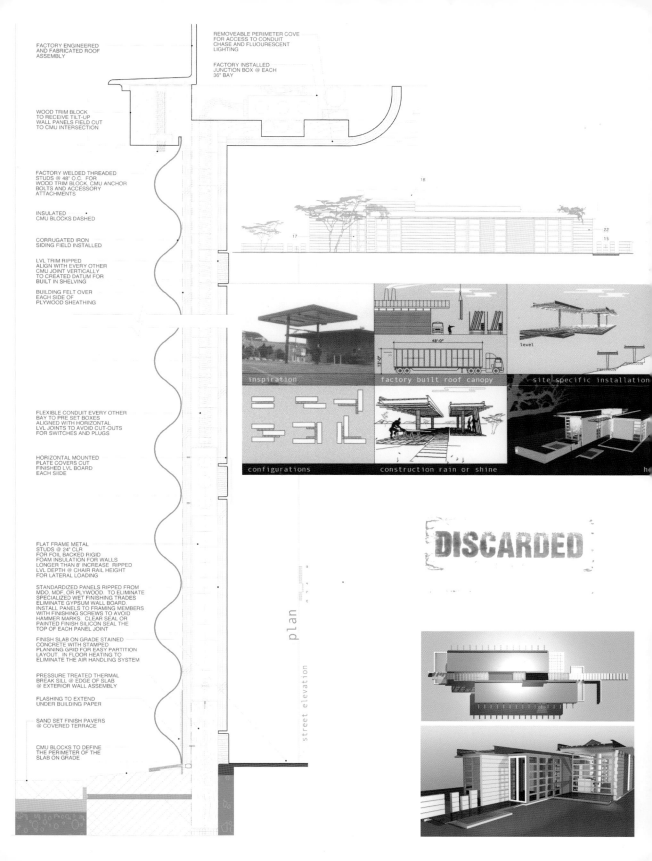

FACTORY ENGINEERED
AND FABRICATED ROOF
ASSEMBLY

REMOVEABLE PERIMETER COVE
FOR ACCESS TO CONDUIT
CHASE AND FLUOURESCENT
LIGHTING

FACTORY INSTALLED
JUNCTION BOX @ EACH
36" BAY

WOOD TRIM BLOCK
TO RECEIVE TILT-UP
WALL PANELS FIELD CUT
TO CMU INTERSECTION

FACTORY WELDED THREADED
STUDS @ 48" O.C. FOR
WOOD TRIM BLOCK. CMU ANCHOR
BOLTS AND ACCESSORY
ATTACHMENTS

INSULATED
CMU BLOCKS DASHED

CORRUGATED IRON
SIDING FIELD INSTALLED

LVL TRIM RIPPED
ALIGN WITH EVERY OTHER
CMU JOINT VERTICALLY
TO CREATED DATUM FOR
BUILT IN SHELVING

BUILDING FELT OVER
EACH SIDE OF
PLYWOOD SHEATHING

FLEXIBLE CONDUIT EVERY OTHER
BAY TO PRE SET BOXES
ALIGNED WITH HORIZONTAL
LVL JOINTS TO AVOID CUT-OUTS
FOR SWITCHES AND PLUGS

HORIZONTAL MOUNTED
PLATE COVERS CUT
FINISHED LVL BOARD
EACH SIIDE

FLAT FRAME METAL
STUDS @ 24" CLR
FOR FOIL BACKED RIGID
FOAM INSULATION FOR WALLS
LONGER THAN 8' INCREASE RIPPED
LVL DEPTH @ CHAIR RAIL HEIGHT
FOR LATERAL LOADING

STANDARDIZED PANELS RIPPED FROM
MDO, MDF, OR PLYWOOD. TO ELIMINATE
SPECIALIZED WET FINISHING TRADES
ELIMINATE GYPSUM WALL BOARD.
INSTALL PANELS TO FRAMING MEMBERS
WITH FINISHING SCREWS TO AVOID
HAMMER MARKS. CLEAR SEAL OR
PAINTED FINISH SILICON SEAL THE
TOP OF EACH PANEL JOINT

FINISH SLAB ON GRADE STAINED
CONCRETE WITH STAMPED
PLANNING GRID FOR EASY PARTITION
LAYOUT. IN FLOOR HEATING TO
ELIMINATE THE AIR HANDLING SYSTEM

PRESSURE TREATED THERMAL
BREAK SILL @ EDGE OF SLAB
@ EXTERIOR WALL ASSEMBLY

FLASHING TO EXTEND
UNDER BUILDING PAPER

SAND SET FINISH PAVERS
@ COVERED TERRACE

CMU BLOCKS TO DEFINE
THE PERIMETER OF THE
SLAB ON GRADE

plan

street elevation

inspiration

factory built roof canopy

site specific installation

configurations

construction rain or shine

he

DISCARDED

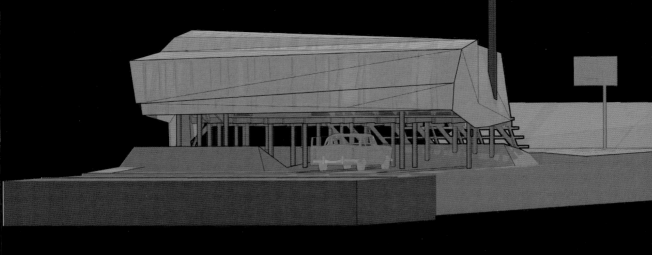

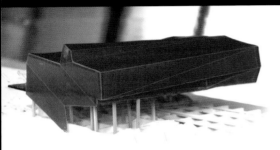

Axonometric System

Douglas Gauthier, Jeremy Edmiston
SYSTEMarchitects
New York, New York

Exploded Axonometric Systems Diagram
Not to Scale

Insulated Skin Sprayed-on polyeurea over an R35 spray-foam.

Gashed Openings Clearstory openings are insulated plastic, vented openings are metal vents and the entry facade is made up of wood and glass doors with fixed non-operable glass wall.

Ribbed Structure
Woven plywood structure with steel joints at each intersection.

Program
Rear of the house has three bedrooms with a toilet, bath and laundry. The large area is divided into living, kitchen and dining zones. Everything is fronted with a deck system.

Stairs
Entry is made from a stairway that connects the undercroft parking to the deck where the main entrance is between the living and kitchen zones.

Foundation & Columns
Treated wood 4"x4" point columns on poured concrete foundations.

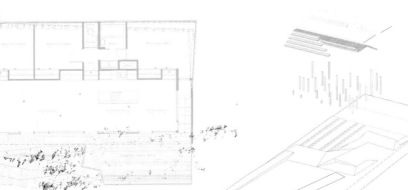

Flood Plain

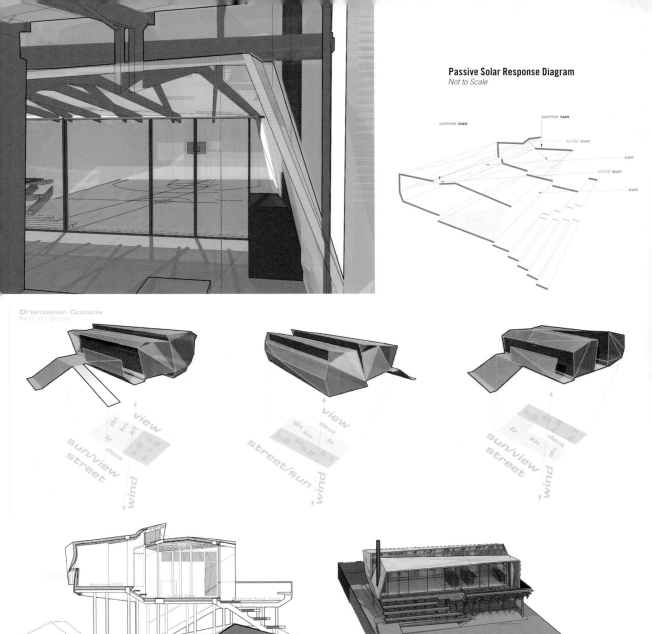

Passive Solar Response Diagram
Not to Scale

summer **sun**

summer **sun**

winter **sun**

sun

winter **sun**

sun

Orientation Options
Not to Scale

view

deck

lv

b.3

b.1

sun/view

street

wind

view

deck

dn kn

lv

b.3

b.1

street/sun

wind

b.3

b.1

lv

deck

kn

sun/view

street

wind

Detail CrossSection

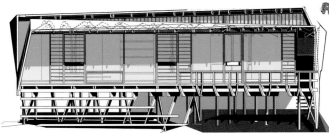

Sun/View Elevation

Porch House

Daniela Fabricius
Brooklyn, New York

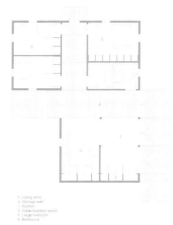

1. Living area
2. Storage wall
3. Kitchen
4. Indoor/outdoor porch
5. Large bedroom
6. Bedrooms

America's last, and most famous, public attempt to re-think the affordable house was the Case Study Houses program of 1945. The program came out of a post-war mentality in which the power of American industry played a major role. The results, though progressive in terms of design, were unrealistic for what the average American desired or could afford. What has changed since 1945?

The Porch House attempts to reflect the economic and cultural conditions in which affordable housing will be built today.

Suburbia by-pass: While the suburban model still dominates home construction in America, both stylistically and organizationally, the Porch House bypasses the suburbs, linking urban and rural models. From the city it borrows the loft-style apartment and elements of modern design. From the rural the dogtrot and cracker style house, and the use of raw, unfinished materials.

Porch: A staple of the southern vernacular house. An extension of the house into the landscape, and into the neighborhood. The inside-out porch is both a path and a resting place. The porch is the stem from which addition and extensions of the house will grow.

Home Depot: The popularity and ubiquitous presence of Home Depot reflects a growing consumer interest in building and DIY projects. Home Depot represents the generic array of materials available to the average American home builder. This is not viewed as a constraint, but as an inspiring game of "making-do". Working with easily obtained materials encourages tinkering and play on the part of the home-owner, and makes repairs easier.

Sustainability: Designed with a warmer climate in mind, the Porch House is fully ventilated from front to back. Bedrooms are better insulated for colder nights, and for warmer nights they receive air circulation through ceiling vents to the hallway. Operable ventilation throughout means less reliance on mechanical systems. Designing on a standard 8' module allows for minimal cut-off waste and labor. Almost all materials are unfinished. All materials are natural, recyclable, reusable, and long-lasting. Wood, which is predominant in the house, is still proven to be one of the most energy efficient materials available.

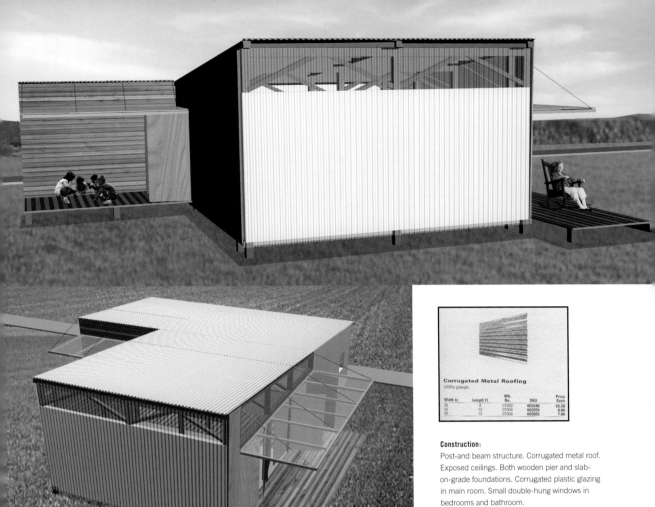

Corrugated Metal Roofing
Utility gauge.

Width In.	Length Ft.	Mfr. No.	SKU	Price Each
26	8	07002	603546	$5.29
26	10	07004	603554	6.99
26	12	07006	603562	7.96

Construction:
Post-and beam structure. Corrugated metal roof.
Exposed ceilings. Both wooden pier and slab-
on-grade foundations. Corrugated plastic glazing
in main room. Small double-hung windows in
bedrooms and bathroom.

Square footage:
Interior living space: 996 sf
Interior porch spaces: 267 sf
Outdoor porch spaces: 376 sf
Total porch space: 643 sf

Estimated materials budget: $20,000 - $25,000
Estimated total budget: $40,000

Elevations

Module M & A

Mario Gentile, Andrew Hart, Reed Crittenden
Brooklyn, New York

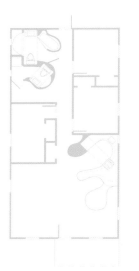

Empowerment through the security, pride, and stability inherent in home ownership is the most important result of Habitat for Humanities' endeavors. Although the organization is primarily dependent upon volunteer labor and donations it is also dependent upon specialized and licensed trades. Two pre-manufactured modules (kitchen "M" and bathrooms "A") will limit the involvement of on site specialized trades, i.e. plumbing and electric. These truckable, infrastructural modules, constructed of a recycled paper core and finished with a polyester resin also act structurally to support the roof and allow for flexibility of the facade. The existing model of empowerment is now enhanced further through the flexibility offered by these modules in several ways; the facade can be formed to take advantage of passive climate control techniques or local or donated materials and, the modules offer a flexibility in spatial arrangement to be tailored to the inhabitants requirements. Now not only is the recipient taking ownership of a home but, also has a voice with the design, relieving the family from the social branding inherent in the current model.

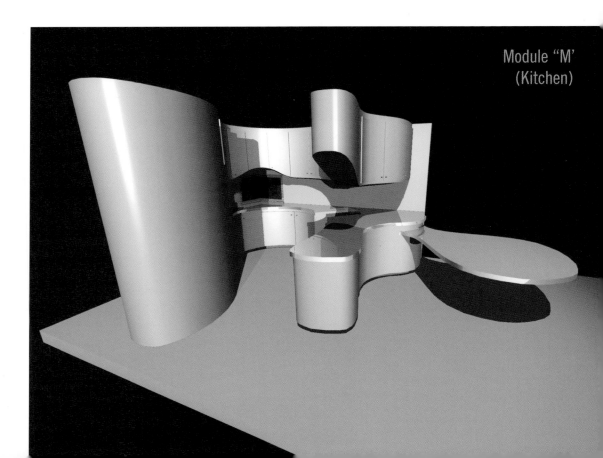

Module "M'
(Kitchen)

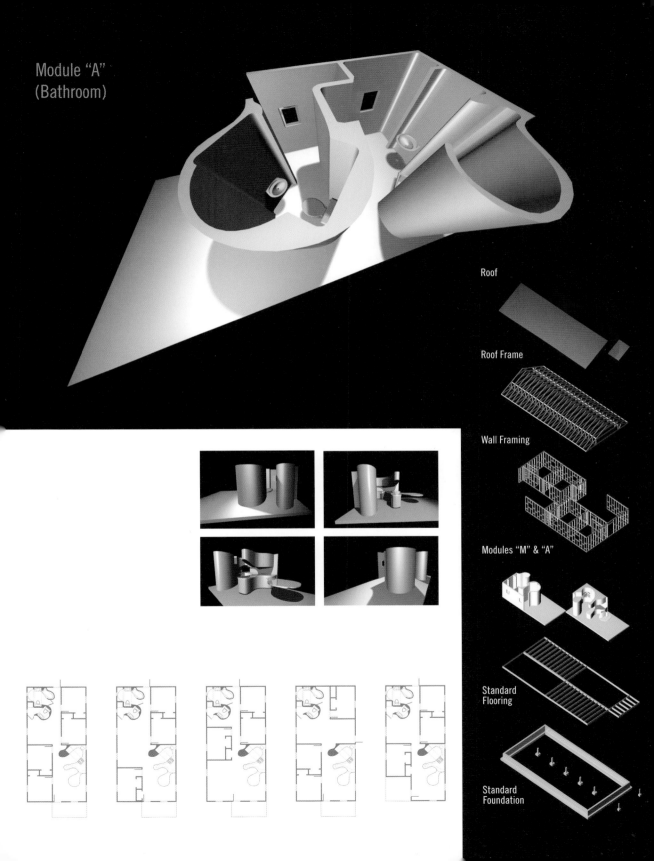

Module "A"
(Bathroom)

Roof

Roof Frame

Wall Framing

Modules "M" & "A"

Standard
Flooring

Standard
Foundation

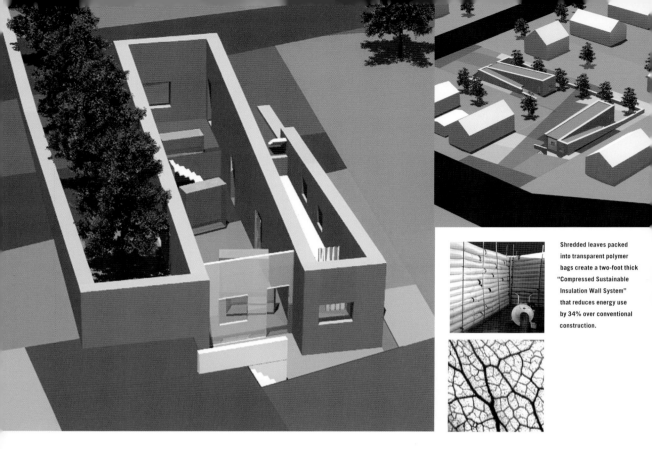

Shredded leaves packed into transparent polymer bags create a two-foot thick "Compressed Sustainable Insulation Wall System" that reduces energy use by 34% over conventional construction.

House of Ivy

Keith Evan Green

School of Architecture
Clemson University
Clemson, South Carolina

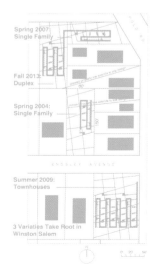

THE HOUSE OF IVY IS NOT A DETACHED HOUSE BUT A GENERATOR WITHIN A LIVING SYSTEM FORMED BY HOUSES, INHABITANTS, THE GROUND AND THE SKY. LIKE IVY ITSELF, THE HOUSE OF IVY IS ACTIVELY GROWING, VARYING, ADAPTING, RENEWING, PHOTOSYNTHESIZING AND ECONOMIZING.

GROWING The location of the HOUSE OF IVY on a typical Winston-Salem lot allows for its incremental growth and eventual duplication. Two units per lot will inevitably be required to accommodate the sustained growth of Winston-Salem's population (29.5% from 1990-2000).

VARYING The basic design for the HOUSE OF IVY yields "varieties" – single units, duplexes and townhouses – as situations demand.

ADAPTING Unlike the conventional detached house, which fails to satisfy a population that is growing older, more childless, more single, the HOUSE OF IVY is a mono-volume space containing mobile furniture that adapts to a multitude of uses, a multitude of lifestyles, a multitude of life transitions. A minimum 26-foot line-of-sight from any location inside the interior makes the 975 square-foot house feel spacious.

RENEWING Towards renewing the suburb's relationship to both urban life and nature, the HOUSE OF IVY is a hybrid: urban and rural – "urbal." "Urban" because it cultivates relationships with other houses through the extension, beyond property lines, of its ivy-like wall and patterned landscaping. "Rural" because it employs vegetation in its construction, it mediates ground and sky (evident in the section drawing), and it replaces the traditional lawn of the suburban dwelling with a low-maintenance native garden.

PHOTOSYNTHESIZING A continuous, bearing wall of leaves readily stores passive solar heat during the day and redistributes it throughout the night. The wall of leaves is finished, inside and out, in stucco, or better, transparent corrugated plastic or transparent polyurethane to reveal the innovative use of the leaves.

ECONOMIZING The materials that make the HOUSE OF IVY can be assembled on site by a supervised volunteer workforce employing simple hand tools. The cost of the house is equivalent to that of a 3-bedroom "Habitat for Humanity" house of conventional design and construction.

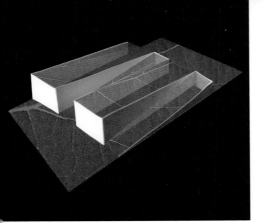

UNLIKE THE CONVENTIONAL "DETACHED" HOUSE THAT FAILS TO ENGAGE ANYTHING AROUND IT OR INSIDE IT, THE HOUSE OF IVY IS ROOTED IN THE PROCESS, NETWORK, CYCLE AND DIVERSITY OF ITS SITUATION. THE HOUSE OF IVY CULTIVATES AN COMMUNITY: A DYNAMIC AND PRODUCTIVE EQUILIBRIUM OF PEOPLE, NATURE AND ARTIFICE.

- Keith Evan Green

Owners 1, 2 and 3 of a single-family unit:

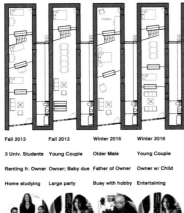

Spring 2004	Spring 2007	Summer 2009	Summer 2009
Young couple	Single male	Single Male	Older Couple
1 child (baby)	Lecturer in Art	Lecturer in Art	Semi-retired
Evening at home	Editing video	Screening videos	Entertaining

The roof is an inhabitable plane extending from the adjoining natural garden. The roof surface, a thin layer of soil and vegetation (over protection board applied to the waterproof membrane) reduces storm water run-off and improves energy performance.

The house's volume is rooted in the earth to gain insulation value from the soil. Openings are placed strategically to maximize ventilation on hot summer days and minimize heat loss during the winter. To add light without adding costly windows, the wall of the entry-façade is constructed of 2"x4" wood studs sheathed in translucent corrugated plastic filled with nontoxic, recycled styrofoam.

Fall 2013	Fall 2013	Winter 2016	Winter 2016
3 Univ. Students	Young Couple	Older Male	Young Couple
Renting fr. Owner	Owner; Baby due	Father of Owner	Owner w/ Child
Home studying	Large party	Busy with hobby	Entertaining

Owner 4 transforms the unit into a duplex after zoning change.

Passive Solar System Design
- Square plan shape minimizes exterior wall area
- Main premises facing South, East and West
- Open floor plan
- Horizontal shading elements on the South wall
- Vertical shading elements on the East and West walls
- Green roof and roof trellis lower the direct heat gain
- Flyash concrete floor to store passive solar heat
- Skylight used as a thermal chimney
- No full-carpet rooms (minimizing moisture holding conditions)
- All operable windows
- Exterior walls insulated with safe natural cotton fiber insulation

Passive Solar Design

Rado Ivanov
Studio R22
Alexandria, Virginia

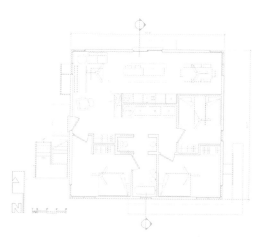

The challenge of the competition was to provide a three-bedroom residence within less than a thousand square feet while maintaining the principles of sustainable design.

To maximize the effectiveness of the layout I chose a square footprint. This eliminated the need for long corridors while at the same time minimizes the amount of exterior walls, and therefore, the heat gains and losses.

All living spaces have east, south, or west exposure, ensuring natural sunlight in each room for at least part of the day. Proper shading is provided by a series of trellises designed to create a deciduous green screen.

The flat roof, accessible by an exterior stair, is an extension to the living space. Roof landscaping provides protection from overheating and minimizes the storm water run-off.

Overall, the residence provides an economical housing solution for an average family without compromising sustainability or lifestyle.

The design of the competition entry was driven by two major factors – an effective floor layout to accommodate the program requirements and the principles of passive solar design

60'-0"

Landscaping
- Tall deciduous trees on the south side of the house
- Evergreen plants at the northeast corner provide privacy and wind screen
- Specially provided trellises for growth of English ivy, and other deciduous vines
- Ground cover: Ophiopogon-Mondo Grass, a small clumping grass-like perennial. Spreads to form a carpet. Drought resistant. Tolerates most soils, sun or shade.
- Landscaped roof

summer sun

future reflected light

winter sun

1' 0 2' 4' 6'

SECTION

Lighting and Energy Conservation
- Energy Star appliances
- Programmable thermostat
- Ceiling fans in living room, dining room, and all bedrooms
- Compact fluorescent lamps in all fixtures
- Low flow shower head
- Green roof minimizes rain water run-off
- Clothes line
- Comfortable outdoor living space
- Heat pump and air conditioner must be within half ton of design capacity
- All ducts are in conditioned space
- Slab on grade fully insulated with close-cell polystyrene foam panels
- Tankless water heater saves some 50% on energy
- Water heater located close to bathroom and kitchen to minimize water waste
- Insulated PEX tubing plumbing using manifold supply system.

Sustainable Material and Methods
- Metal framing and trellises with bolted connection for future disassembly
- Dark color patterned flyash concrete floor
- Fiber-cement exterior tile cladding
- Thermo-ply insulated exterior wall sheathing with aluminum radiant barrier
- All interior wall board made of by-product gypsum and recycled paper
- Low-E, double paned, gas-filled windows
- Voids around all windows and doors to be insulated with backer rods
- Low VOC paint and interior adhesives and caulks
- Minimized construction waste with 16", 24", 48" plan dimensions

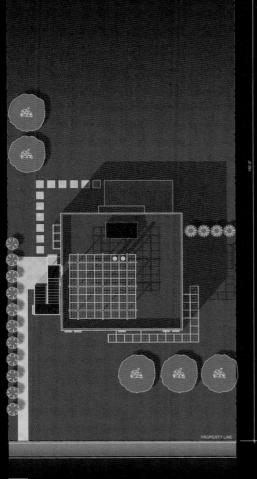

PROPERTY LINE

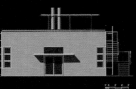
N

2' 0 4' 6' 12'

SITE PLAN

Project Data

Total Indoor Area	1,024 s.f.
Number of Bedrooms	Three
Number of Bathrooms	One (w/ two compartments)
Carport/Garage	None

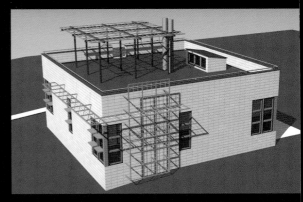

NORTH ELEVATION

WEST ELEVATION

SOUTH ELEVATION

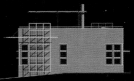
EAST ELEVATION

Fab Tree Hab

Mitchell Joachim, Lara Greden, Javier Arbona

Team H.E.D. (Human Ecology Design)
MIT School of Architecture
Cambridge, Massachusetts

The Fab Tree Hab

The living structure single-family home and encompassing ecology. Tree trunks from the load-bearing structure to which a weave of pleached branch 'studs' support a thermal clay and straw-based infill. The Fab Tree Hab plan accommodates three bedrooms (one on the second level), a bathroom, and an open living, dining and kitchen area placed on the southern façade in accordance with passive solar principles.

Structure, form, and growth

A methodology new to buildings yet ancient to gardening is introduced in this design - pleaching. Pleaching is a method of weaving together tree branches to form living archways, lattices, or screens. The trunks of inosculate, or self-grafting, trees, such as Elm, Live Oak, and Dogwood, are the load-bearing structure, and the branches form a continuous lattice frame for the walls and roof. Weaved along the exterior is a dense protective layer of vines, interspersed with soil pockets and growing plants. On the interior, a clay and straw composite insulates and blocks moisture, and a final layer of smooth clay is applied like a plaster to dually provide comfort and aesthetics.

Rethinking budget

At the first stage of maturity, when the habitat is readied for human presence, cost outlays are similar in nature to traditional construction, yet much less in magnitude based on their local, natural, and edible qualities. Clay, gravel, and straw can be obtained locally for certainly no more than the cost of concrete. Plants and vegetation, many of which can be started from seedlings when the structure is originally planted, will come at a nominal cost. Installation of heating, lighting, plumbing, electrical, and communication systems will be no more than that for a typical home, and should be less due to the systems integrated design of natural ventilation, gravity water flow, daylighting and passive solar. As illustrated by this comparative assessment, realization of a living home certainly fits within the realm of affordability.

Experiment in time

Above all, the raising of this home can be achieved at a minimal price, requiring only some time to complete its structure. Realization of these homes will begin as an experiment, and it is envisioned that thereafter, the concept of renewal will take on a new architectural form - one of interdependency between nature and people.

1. Rain Harvester
2. Flexible Bioplastic Windows
3. Living Machine
Purification System
4. Clean Water
5. Pleached Wall
6. Live Elm Superstructure

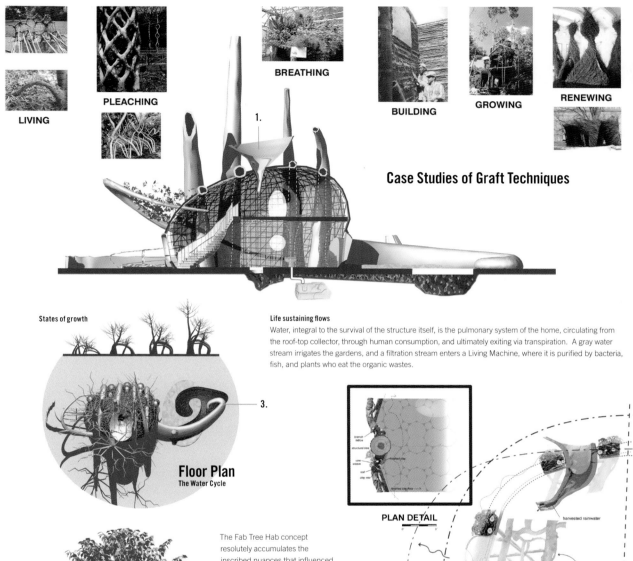

LIVING

PLEACHING

BREATHING

BUILDING

GROWING

RENEWING

1.

Case Studies of Graft Techniques

States of growth

3.

Floor Plan
The Water Cycle

Life sustaining flows

Water, integral to the survival of the structure itself, is the pulmonary system of the home, circulating from the roof-top collector, through human consumption, and ultimately exiting via transpiration. A gray water stream irrigates the gardens, and a filtration stream enters a Living Machine, where it is purified by bacteria, fish, and plants who eat the organic wastes.

PLAN DETAIL

harvested rainwater

transpiratory cooling

gray water feeds garden

window opens to receive breeze

radiant heating coils

rammed earth pavers

gravel bed

thermal mass

WALL SECTION SOUTHERN FACADE
THE VENTILATION & HEATING CYCLES

The Fab Tree Hab concept resolutely accumulates the inscribed nuances that influenced the American Rustic period. Stemming form the insurgent writings of Thoreau, Emerson, Whitman, and Alcott, America defined a sensibility. These authors represent an early mode of intention that was profoundly ecocentric. Their notion of dwelling was envisioned as retreats, poets' bowers, hermitages, and summer cottages in a Sylvan style. In 1847 it culminated in the self-made assembly of a crooked cedar and honeysuckle summer home by Thoreau and Alcott for their friend Emerson in the midst of a cornfield. This peculiar house severed as our point of departure.

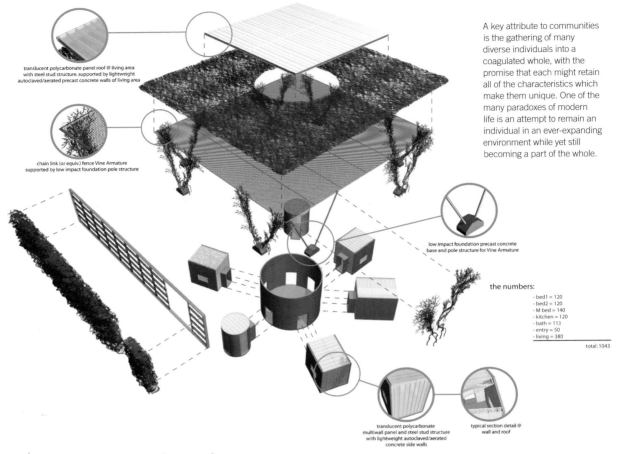

translucent polycarbonate panel roof @ living area with steel stud structure. supported by lightweight autoclaved/aerated precast concrete walls of living area

chain link (or equiv.) fence Vine Armature supported by low impact foundation pole structure

A key attribute to communities is the gathering of many diverse individuals into a coagulated whole, with the promise that each might retain all of the characteristics which make them unique. One of the many paradoxes of modern life is an attempt to remain an individual in an ever-expanding environment while yet still becoming a part of the whole.

low impact foundation precast concrete base and pole structure for Vine Armature

the numbers:
- bed1 = 120
- bed2 = 120
- M bed = 140
- kitchen = 120
- bath = 113
- entry = 50
- living = 380

total: 1043

translucent polycarbonate multiwall panel and steel stud structure with lightweight autoclaved/aerated concrete side walls

typical section detail @ wall and roof

The Heterogeneous Community

Joseph Karadin
Forest Hills, New York

Our homes are micro communities, each with an agora (living area), a restaurant (kitchen and dining room), a bath house (bathroom), a park (garden) and a triumphal arch (entry). At the core is the place where we live the most, where we sit, relax and interact, eat and drink, and entertain ourselves. Adjacent to this is where we clean ourselves, sleep and kick off our shoes. The way we live can be the model of where we live. Walls of varying opacities at the entrance to our houses make an indirect (or direct) statement of our desire to be private. They separate the many layers of privacy and publicity from the entrance (most public) to the back yard (most private) and everything in between. But this "Billboard" is more than just a divider partition, it can be the unifying element within the community that can also become a "differentiator" to the individual homeowner, simply by changing color, material, texture or any other possible attribute ("my house is the one with the big red wall").

Behind this screen is where the real interaction takes place. Each home can be the same but different; the basic structure is the same i.e. materials construction, etc. (as it is now with current construction methods) but the object forms can take on any shape and any juxtaposition. For natural cooling and general protection from the elements, each home has a living vine-covered roof, which among many things can aid in slowing the velocity of rain and wind on each module, planted with a wide variety of fast growing vines and is supported by a low-impact pole foundation. Each module of the home is constructed of two primary materials: lightweight autoclaved/aerated fiber reinforced concrete and polycarbonate translucent dimensional multiwall panels supported by steel stud wall structure. This dichotomy between solidity and lightness helps to balance the feeling of containment and openness (lightness).

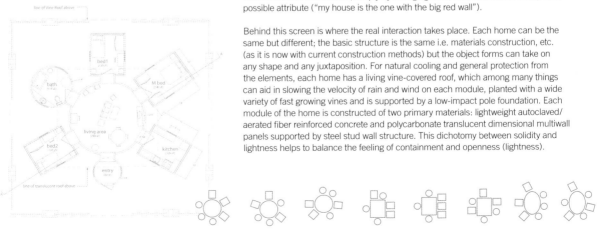

One of the many ways in which we find our outward "identities" is through the things we possess; our clothing, our cars, our houses, etc. all of which are manufactured on a massive scale, occasionally catered to our desire to be unique with a color change, or a change in material. With this understood, how can our everyday environments become a catalyst for our compulsion to be different?

top perspective

detail at Vine Roof structure base

With the ability to form our homes to the way in which we live (as opposed to changing they way in which we live to fit our homes) we can create homogeneous communities which retain our individual "identities" and maintain our privacy and the need for shared interaction.

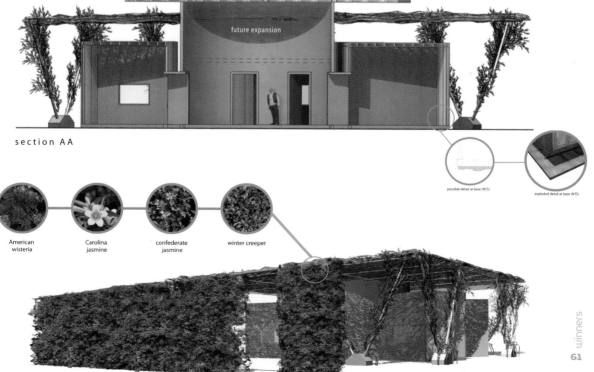

future expansion

section AA

possible detail at base (NTS)

exploded detail at base (NTS)

American wisteria

Carolina jasmine

confederate jasmine

winter creeper

winners

front perspective

Large/Less Strategy

Kenneth Kim, Paula Rosales, Wojtek Sosnowski
MOREMAS
New York, New York

Use of largest and lightest materials, within physical and economic feasibility, results in large/ less pieces that equals less time, the fundamentals of construction economics.

At the center of the large/ less strategy, is a truss structure developed to replace conventional masonry or 2x construction with a larger modular unit. The trusses can be made of wood, steel, or be a hybrid. They are easily modified into different configurations and sizes for each house, with a different roof, and sheathing or infill material. More importantly, the truss can be prefabricated and delivered to a jobsite and erected in one day reducing the amount of workdays in the field. The truss also eliminates almost all foundation work and makes it adaptable to any site condition. The truss sets the precedent for everything else in the construction. This is the concept of the building.

Straw bale, from an economic position, is an ideal material for enclosure. It is inexpensive, light, easy to install with unskilled labor, and big. From an ecological perspective, they represent large blocks of a very fast renewable resource. Straw is actually considered a waste product in agriculture. In this proposal for a site in Winston-Salem, North Carolina, straw bale makes up 3/4 of all the exterior walls set in a glulam truss super structure, replacing conventional materials.

Other than the truss, the other materials are replaceable by what is available. In this manner, the building will change in appearance and configuration from case to case. Influenced by site and materials available or affordable, the construction logic of the building will depend on the properties of those materials selected. In general, green materials and environmentally friendly materials, are to be utilized wherever but only whenever efficiently applicable. Steel is accepted as a material primarily because it is very strong and can span large distances with less material.

Depending on the site, extensive passive heating and/ or cooling principles are incorporated into the design. The Winston-Salem house will have at least passive water heaters, or solar power for water heaters. The plastered straw bale construction acts a good insulator and the concrete slab acts as a thermal mass. Tall rooms with good ventilation are introduced to create a heat chimney. The rainwater is collected in a cistern below grade, and can either be used solely for gray water systems, or depending on the budget be adapted with filters for potable water. Exterior doors and shutters provide sunshade, additional insulation, and hurricane protection at this site.

interior view of living and dining

view with sun shades open

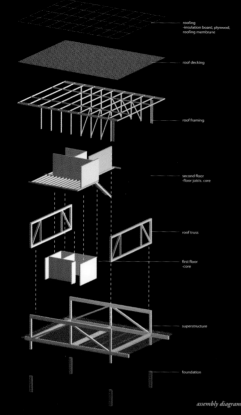

roofing
-insulation board, plywood,
roofing membrane

roof decking

roof framing

second floor
-floor joists core

roof truss

first floor
-core

superstructure

foundation

assembly diagram

view with sun shades closed

As an alternative, the concept house is a hybrid, relying mostly on passive heating and cooling design, some solar power hot water, and the grid. North Carolina, as well as 13 other states, currently has alternative sources of clean energy. For an additional fee (approximately $4/month), customers subsidize the local government's programs that introduce methane gas electricity, solar, hydro, and other renewable sources of energy. If Habitat for Humanity can dedicate just $2,000 from the construction budget towards such subsidy programs, it is promoting green energy at a macro level for approximately 40 years ($4/mo.x12mo.x40yrs=$1,920). If these programs are successful, they could one day replace all conventional power plants that currently pollute our environment, and even reduce the cost of utilities, truly an ultimate large/ less strategy. This is a macro policy that has the potential to make a more significant impact than converting every individual home into a standalone system.

Lastly, in anticipation of the unknown future, the house is flexible and can be easily accessible for modifications, since it is already designed elevated off the ground. If budget and site conditions permit, the house can be fitted for extensive solar, hydro, wind, and geothermal systems at a later date. Regardless of what the future holds, thinking large/ less is a good strategy. For this competition, our building prototype is then not so much the building proposal, but rather a strategy.

view of entry - south elevation

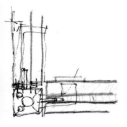

Foundations are pre-assembled Screwjack© systems which eliminate the need for costly engineered foundations, and simplify the construction process by eliminating the need for level surveying prior to building the floor deck. During construction, the floor plate can be installed and leveled prior to further framing and wall installation with either a transit or a long stick level. In the event of foundation heave or settlement, the jacks are simply adjusted by turning a large nut on a 1-1/2" stainless steel threaded bearing rod.

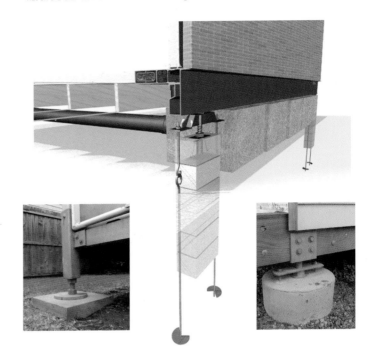

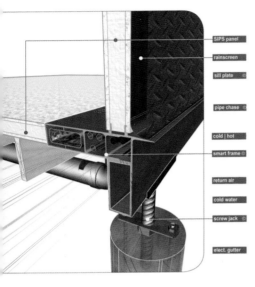

- SIPS panel
- rainscreen
- sill plate
- pipe chase ©
- cold | hot
- smart frame ©
- return air
- cold water
- screw jack ©
- elect. gutter

FrameWork

Joe Meppelink, Adam Janusz, Onezieme Mouton, Wyatt Frantom

Framework
Houston, Texas

As with any system, process, or prototypical development in the arena of affordable housing, FRAMEWORK realizes that a sense of place, cultural identity, and pride in ownership is required for unilateral success. The cold efficiency of notorious projects such as Pruitt-Igoe and Cabrini Green are testament to such failures, despite the best intentions of their notable designers (Minoru Yamasaki, and Lawrence Armstadter, respectively) to provide Corbusian cities of tomorrow.

The current mode of affordable housing development is problematic in that it finds the lowest common denominator in quality of materials and construction, and blindly deploys these "standards" to create faux-historic vernaculars often inappropriate to their contexts.

FRAMEWORK provides a clean minimal structural system of anodized aluminum framing and painted SIP panels, with a customized flair of colored automotive-finished roof forms, and anodized aluminum finish on the frame. The house could be quickly assembled by trained technicians, and could also be built using unskilled volunteer labor due to its simple components and minimal need of power tool use. Flanges are also provided on the exterior perimeter extrusions that allow for addition of finish materials which further customize and project the will of the owners and their abilities and aesthetic choices, and also create a beneficial rain-screen system which will even further improve R-values in the walls and extend the life of the exterior envelope.

The concept utilizes the sectional flexibility of extruded aluminum in combination with the planar flexibility of structural insulated panels (SIPs). SIPS, used here for walls, floor and a customized form of roofing, have nearly twice the R-values of conventional building methods, R-18 walls and R-36 roof. The heating and cooling works naturally with convection currents for added efficiency. The extruded aluminum frame, called Smartframe©, is a multi-cellular aluminum extrusion which carries cold air, hot and cold water, electrical, and data utilities within its profiles. The Smartframe© members are profiled to interlock and create a semi-rigid frame. SIPS are then "dropped" into the Smartframe© and serve as a pre-finished wall panel or a sub-structure for additional finishes.

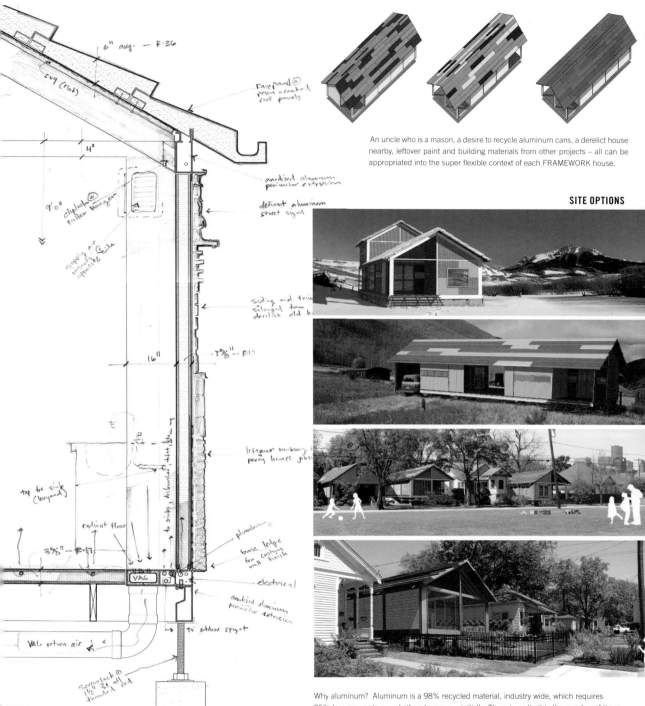

6" avg. – R-36

2x9 (flat)

rainpond @ resin-coated roof panels

anodized aluminum perimeter extrusion

4"

9'0" cliplock @ rafter hangers

supply at lowest @ opposite side

defunct aluminum street signs

Siding and trim salvaged from derelict old h...

16"

3⅝" – R-17

leftover masonry @ perry homes jobsite

tap for sink (beyond)

radiant floor

3⅝" – R-17

plumbing

base ledge for custom wall finish

electrical

anodized aluminum perimeter extrusion

VAC

VAC return air

to outdoor spigot

screwjack @ 1½" set off threaded rod

An uncle who is a mason, a desire to recycle aluminum cans, a derelict house nearby, leftover paint and building materials from other projects – all can be appropriated into the super flexible context of each FRAMEWORK house.

SITE OPTIONS

Why aluminum? Aluminum is a 98% recycled material, industry wide, which requires 95% less energy to recycle than to process initially. There is no limit to the number of times aluminum can be reclaimed, so the metal we use here will last a lifetime.

SECTION DIAGRAMS

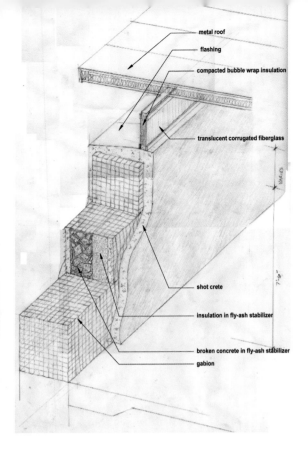

- metal roof
- flashing
- compacted bubble wrap insulation
- translucent corrugated fiberglass
- shot crete
- insulation in fly-ash stabilizer
- broken concrete in fly-ash stabilizer
- gabion

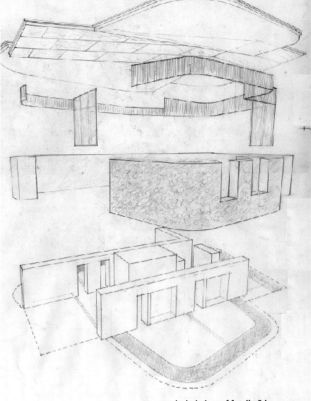

exploded view of family 2 house

Gabion House

Mark Nye
Lambertville, New Jersey

FAMILY #1
4BR HOUSE
1130 S.F.
scale: 1/8"=1'-0"

The quality of mass single family housing will not be improved until a balance is struck between the specificity of each inhabitant and the standardized parts that make mass housing possible.

This proposal will interpret the American values of community, individualism, and practicality in three distinct representations.

The act of replacing driveways alone results in 13,000,000 tons of refuse each year., Over a third of the debris generated by residential renovations. A fresh review of the ancient technique of rubble wall construction provides a new use for this rubbish. The method of construction proposed with each of these projects consists of gabions, wire mesh baskets, filled with concrete rubble and a section of insulation, stacked and sprayed with shot-crete.

These units are assembled on site to the specifications of each family. Meanwhile, standardized cabinetry elements form the bulk of the interior separation. My estimate is that the cost of this construction system is around $40.00 Per square foot.

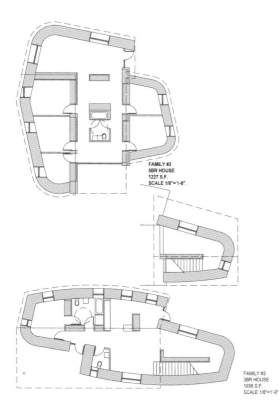

FAMILY #2
5BR HOUSE
1227 S.F.
SCALE 1/8"=1'-0".

FAMILY #3
3BR HOUSE
1036 S.F.
SCALE 1/8"=1'-0"

interior view of family 3 house

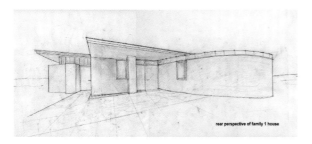

rear perspective of family 1 house

Family 1

Single mother with one daughter and two sons. Her eldest is also a single mother with a newborn. She and the baby live in a separate wing and the sons continue to share a room. The mother works as a hospital admin and has arranged to work half time at home. The daughter currently waitresses while also taking some classes at a local community college. Once she is able to move out on her own, her mother intends to convert the second bedroom in the wing to a bathroom. Their lifestyle is best characterized as informal. From the mother's perspective, a house must be practical and easy to maintain.

Family 2

Immigrant family of three with a live-in mother-in-law. The husband is a part-time security officer and the wife is a full-time bookkeeper at a local small business. They both hope to start their own landscaping business when they have saved enough money. The mother-in-law assists with the daily tasks and watches the baby while the parents are working. The husband's brother is also staying at the house until he obtains his green card. This family wants a house that both evokes their native land and also represents values of their newly adopted country.

Family 3

The mother of this family of three is a pastor at the local church and the father is an elementary school teacher. A twelve year old daughter from the father's first marriage comes to stay with them on weekends. The parents are active in the community and the mother, as pastor, often conducts prayer meetings and counsels individuals at home. This couple is interested in a house that is inspiring and speaks to traditional values.

Adapt (home)

Drura Parrish
London, England and Henderson, Kentucky

ADAPT (home) is network of components that fuse to create a habitat. This network begins with the framework of design and ends with installation. This involves a simple system of supply, manufacture, and installation. In order to cut costs, it is preferred to have a larger entity buying materials and supplies in bulk. This enterprise becomes the facilitator of goods for manufacture. By focusing manufacture, an opportunity is created to provide a place for employment and education. Idealist in stance, this logic aids in the issue of affordable housing. There are socioeconomic factors at play that have brought the need for this title. By going beyond the end means, the process of creating a house for one becomes the provider for a few or many. This point of manufacture supports the community in which it may create. Manufacturing these supplies is compiled into a module for its ease of transportation and installation, eliminating waste from heavy on-site construction and transportation pollution.

A modular system was chosen simply because no one situation is alike. Tremendous waste occurs through outward expansion from city centers. Instead of focusing on new construction, it is important to imagine a possible application that can apply across the board from rural areas to downtowns.

There are four primary elements in ADAPT (home). First is the utility trailer, which seeks to assist and sustain existing central or remote conditions, as well as new construction. The trailer is meant to serve as a starting point in energy efficiency. A supplemental solar skin is second, where it serves to supplement the trailer, as well as providing structural reinforcement in existing buildings. Third is the primary building module, which serves as livable space in both additions and new construction. Last, is an interior wall system that allows for instant layout customization by the user of the final achieved space.

Overall costs are also efficient due to the power of scale. Element use is situation specific, not all are used in every condition. Estimated costs for the solar skin are relatively high ($1,200 per 2'x8' panel), but gains in efficiency and utility savings counter in the long run. The trailer cost is estimated at $3,500 without appliances, however, it is meant to supplement and may be taken away once use is not needed. The primary building module (64 sq.ft.) is estimated to cost $17 dollars per sq. ft. without roof. Roofing options (64 sq. ft. each) vary from daylighting ($1,700), solar ($1,400), and green roof ($110). The interior wall system is estimated to cost $20 per lineal foot. For approximately $40,000, a three bedroom 1,150 sq. ft home could be constructed.

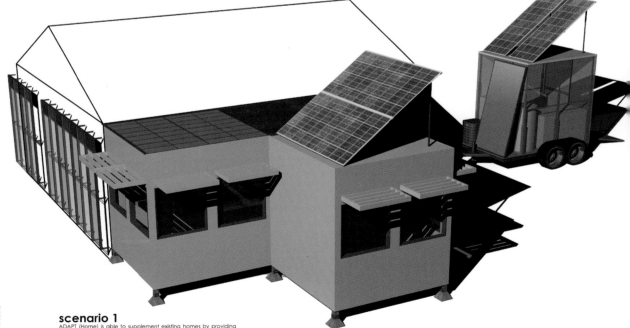

scenario 1
ADAPT (Home) is able to supplement existing homes by providing environmental building elements and efficient utility plug-ins. By reclaiming smaller urban and rural homes for rehabilitation, demolition and construction waste can be minimized. This, in turn aids the sustainability of the construction cycle, as well as the rehabilitation of existing less advantaged neighborhoods. Shown is a hypothetical addition of 192 sq. ft. to a 645 sq. ft. home, with three modules, solar skin for increased electric production and support, as well as a utility trailer.

scenario 2

New construction can be carried out easily and efficiently. By concentrating module construction off-site, on-site construction pollution is minimized through easy installation. The modules can be replicated vertically and horizontally to achieve desired size, and the interior wall system can be adjusted for layout. Customization takes place by the user in the form of roof, exterior color, and interior wall covering. One of the goals of the ADAPT (home) is to maximize size and customization through the isolation and standardization of its parts. Layout designation, such as bathroom, kitchen, bedroom, etc., is at choosing of the user. Appliances and cabinetry are separate items for easy installation to be "plugged" into the new construction.

Emphasis has been put on existing and upcoming sustainable materials within these elements. Primary structural components are either parallel strand lumber (PSL), steel or fast growing aspen I beam joists. Steel is readily one of the most recyclable of materials, while PSL reclaims and recycles otherwise wasted wood product.

Structurally insulated panels comprised of light gauge steel construction and modified expanded polystyrene (EPS) were chosen for exterior walls for their strength and high R values (R=33), as well as no need for extra material for sheathing, vapor, or moisture barriers. Windows are double glazed and UV coated for optimal performance.

Fiber cement serves as siding without asbestos, fiberglass or harmful chemicals. Polycarbonate panels are in the interior wall system and trailer for lightness, durability, and re-usability. Gas filled panels (GFP) are the insulation for the interior wall system, providing maximum flexibility, lightness, sound buffering, and insulation (R=28).

Aerogels are used in the daylighting roof for their low weight, light transmission and insulation properties (R=20). Green roofing is also used to maximize low cost thermal efficiency, as well as possibilities for a gray water system.

Pin foundations are used for low site construction and impact. To conclude, bamboo flooring is used in the interior.

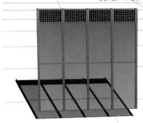

solar wall

building module

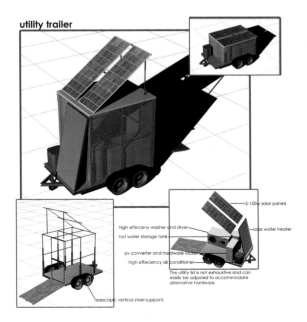

2-4'x8' 150w solar panels over SIPS

2-4'x8' aerogel structural skylight panels with R value of 20

green roof for water collection and thermal properties

parallel strand lumber beams and columns

aspen i-joists

pin foundations

SIPS exterior with R value of 33

bamboo interior flooring

utility trailer

high effecieny washer and dryer

hot water storage tank

pv converter and hardware locker

high effecieny air conditioner

2-150w solar panels

solar water heater

The utility list is not exhaustive and can easily be adjusted to accommodate alternative hardware.

telescopic vertical steel supports

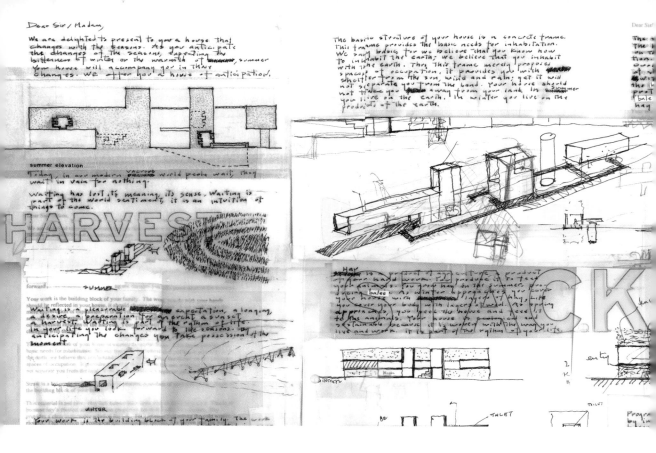

Hay Bale House

Ronald Rael, Patricio del Real
Seneca, South Carolina

We are delighted to present to you a house that changes with the seasons. As you anticipate the changes of the seasons, expecting the bitterness of winter or the warmth of summer your house will accompany you in those changes. We offer you a house of anticipation.

The basic structure of your house is a concrete frame. This frame provides the basic needs for inhabitation. We are basic, for we believe that you know how to inhabit the Earth: We believe that you inhabit with the Earth. Thus this frame merely proposes spaces of occupation. It provides you with shelter from the sun, wind, and rain; yet it will not separate you from the land. Your house should not take you away from your land. In Summer you live on the Earth. In the Winter you live on the products of the Earth.

The house completes itself with the product of your labor, HAY BALE. We are building your house with concrete. You finish your house with an endo-dermis, a mass of hay. In Summer you remove this mass. The house sheds its protective layer.

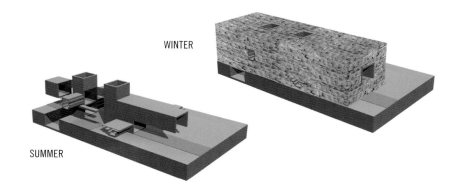

WINTER

SUMMER

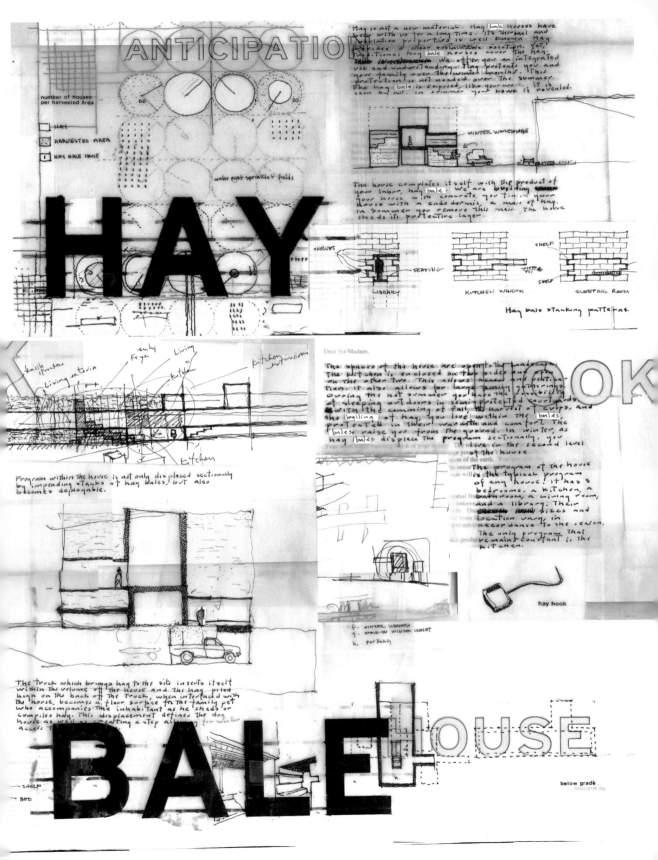

ANTICIPATION

number of houses
per harvested area

60   20

☐ HAY
▦ HARVESTED AREA
◯ HAY BALE HOUSE

center pivot sprinkler fields

Hay is not a new material. Hay bale houses have been with us for a long time. Its thermal and insulation properties is well known. Hay provides a clear sustainable solution. Yet, traditional hay bale houses cover the hay. We offer you an integrated use and understand how hay protects you and your family over the winter months. This protection is not needed over the summer. The hay bale is exposed, like your house — it is seen by all. In summer your house is revealed.

WINTER WARDROBE

The house completes itself with the product of your labor, hay bale. We are building your house with concrete, you finish your house with a endoderm, a mass of hay. In summer you remove this mass. The house sheds its protective layer.

SHELVES
LIBRARY
SEATING

SHELF
KITCHEN WINDOW
SHELF
SLEEPING ROOM

Hay bale stacking patterns.

HAY

sensible furniture
Living area
entry
Foyer
Living
kitchen
kitchen extrusion
kitchen

Program within the house is not only displaced sectionally by impending stacks of hay bales, but also becomes deployable.

Dear Sir/Madam,

The spaces of the house are open to the landscape. The kitchen is enclosed on two sides and open on the other two. This allows access and ventilation, it also allows for large family gatherings. During the hot summer you have the possibility of sleeping outdoors in semi protected courtyards. With the coming of fall, the harvest of crops, and the bailing of hay, you live low within the bales, protected in their warmth and comfort. The bales raise you from the ground. In winter, as hay bales displace the program sectionally, you live in the second level of the house.

The program of the house is the typical program of any house. It has 3 bedrooms, a kitchen, bathrooms, a living room, and a library. Their sizes and location vary in accordance to the season. The only program that remains constant is the kitchen.

LOOK

f. WINTER LIBRARY
g. WALK-IN WINTER CLOSET
h. parking

hay hook

The truck which brings hay to the site inserts itself within the volume of the house and the hay piled high on the back of the truck, when interfaced with the house, becomes a floor surface for the family pet who accompanies the inhabitant as he sheds or compiles hay. This displacement defines the dog house as well as creating a step allowing for winter access.

SHELF
BED

BALE HOUSE

below grade

Adaptive Re-use

Steven Raike

Bear Creek, Pennsylvania

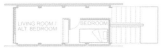

UPPER LEVEL PLAN

SECOND LEVEL PLAN

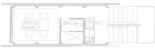

FIRST LEVEL PLAN

The unit of habitation is essentially an adaptive re-use of vacant urban space. It has as its primary goal the provision of upscale housing which is not normally associated with habitat for humanity projects. As its secondary pursuit, the unit of habitation seeks to challenge the typology of the modern day dwelling, as an overt symbol of one's socioeconomic status. Since the structure for the project is already in place, the budget can be allocated to enclosure and finishes that would normally be economically unavailable to a typical habitat home. The enclosure is a series of molded composite modules which have all required electrical and plumbing infrastructure embedded prior to assembly.

In concert with the composite modules, the enclosure is completed by off the shelf aluminum curtain wall components. The unit is entirely independent of city services since it has a photovoltaic collection system on the roof and the elevation which is primarily west facing. Rainwater is collected and stored for domestic use and is purified by osmotic filters.

As an urban response to what is often a suburban building type, the unit of habitation challenges the status quo by adopting not some false visage of style, but by adopting a scrim that changes on a monthly basis. It is impossible to categorize the style of the house since its appearance is in a constant state of flux. Additionally the structure is perched in lofty circles which are typically the province of the rich.

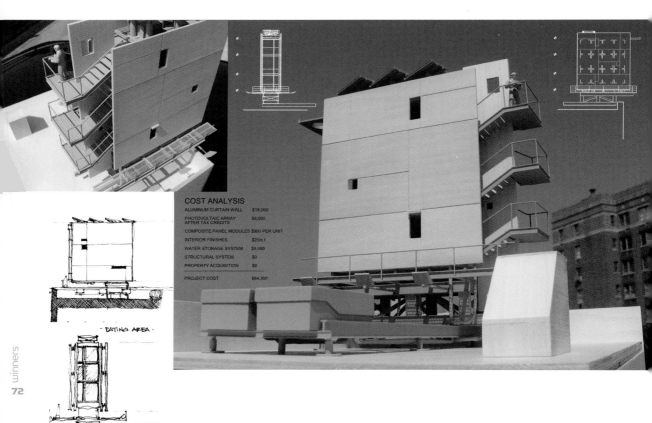

COST ANALYSIS

ALUMINUM CURTAIN WALL	$18,000
PHOTOVOLTAIC ARRAY AFTER TAX CREDITS	$6,000
COMPOSITE PANEL MODULES	$900 PER UNIT
INTERIOR FINISHES	$25/s.f.
WATER STORAGE SYSTEM	$5,000
STRUCTURAL SYSTEM	$0
PROPERTY ACQUISITION	$0
PROJECT COST	$64,300

· EATING AREA ·

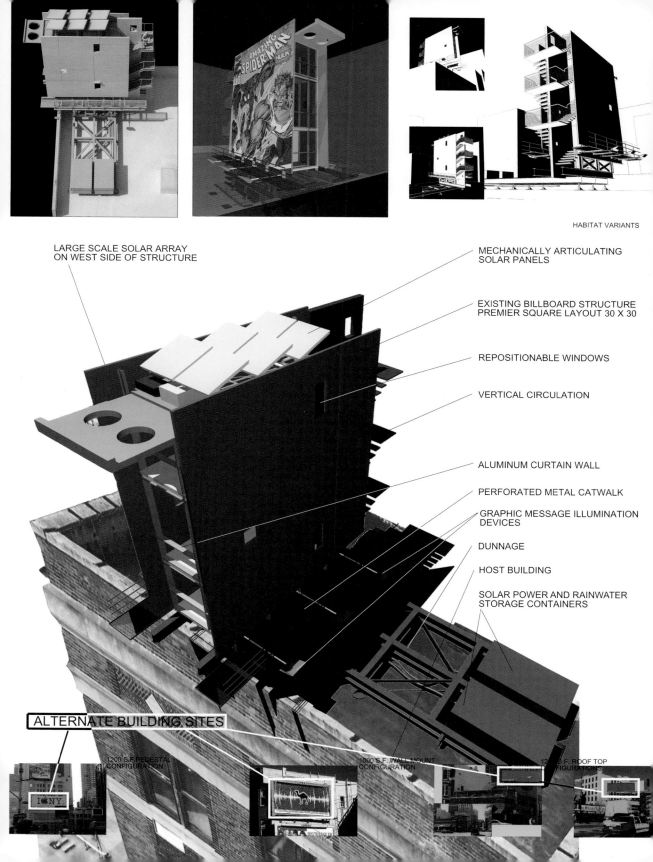

HABITAT VARIANTS

LARGE SCALE SOLAR ARRAY
ON WEST SIDE OF STRUCTURE

MECHANICALLY ARTICULATING
SOLAR PANELS

EXISTING BILLBOARD STRUCTURE
PREMIER SQUARE LAYOUT 30 X 30

REPOSITIONABLE WINDOWS

VERTICAL CIRCULATION

ALUMINUM CURTAIN WALL

PERFORATED METAL CATWALK

GRAPHIC MESSAGE ILLUMINATION
DEVICES

DUNNAGE

HOST BUILDING

SOLAR POWER AND RAINWATER
STORAGE CONTAINERS

ALTERNATE BUILDING SITES

1200 S.F. PEDESTAL
CONFIGURATION

1000 S.F. WALL MOUNT
CONFIGURATION

1200 S.F. ROOF TOP
CONFIGURATION

The length of the **SOUTH FAÇADE** is maximized to improve passive solar benefits for winter heat gain and daylighting. **1** **Carefully calculated roof over-hangs** and a **louvered shading screen** block the high summer sun, yet allow lower winter sun to enter the house. **Operable windows**, on the north and south sides, provide cross ventilation. Super-insulated glass above the light shelf minimizes heat loss. **Water tubes**, used as a thermal mass behind the south glazing, absorb heat throughout the day and release it at night. Cellular **insulated window shades** prevent nighttime heat loss.

SITE CONSIDERATION influ-ences the house's orientation, landscape, and passive solar opportunities. Orienting **2** the house to maximize **southern expo-sure** achieves optimum passive solar benefits. **Preservation of site resources**, such as native trees, is considered in the loca-tion of the house. Additional plantings include deciduous trees on the south to provide summer shade and coniferous trees on the north to provide a north wind buffer. A **north swale**, that will be converted to native grass, blocks winter winds and absorbs run-off.

GREEN MATERIALS and sustainable practices are used to achieve **3** environmentally responsible design. High **fly ash content concrete**, gravel content from crushed concrete, and recycled content insulation and gypsum are used throughout. **Materials salvaged** from area buildings slated for demo-lition, such as **industrial steel windows**, are re-used as high-end materials for little or no cost. **Maple flooring** is re-used from an area gymnasium, in lieu of basic-grade carpet, which is poorer for indoor air quality and recyclability.

GARAGE EMPHASIS is mini-mized with access from the rear, leaving **4** the front of the house to respond to the neighborhood. Focus is aimed at neigh-borhood socialization. The front yard is more **approachable at a pedestrian scale**. In this design, the placement of the garage to the north allows the livable spaces to take advantage of the south exposure for winter heat gain and daylighting. A **grasscrete driveway** replaces concrete to maximize open green space and reduce stormwater runoff, soil erosion, and summer heat gain.

A truly **COST-EFFECTIVE** house continues to be affordable after the occu-pant moves in. **Energy efficiency** and **5** low-maintenance materials contribute to the reduction of the house's life cycle costs. **Low-maintenance materials**, that require less time and money for upkeep, are used in place of paint, which may need reappli-cation. Care with construction waste contributes to the house's cost-effectiveness. **Concrete formwork is reused** for sub-flooring and framing materials. **Regional materials** are used to reduce transportation costs and pollu-tion created in traveling great distances.

STORAGE is maximized throughout the house as an integral part of the **6** architectural aesthetic. **Integrating storage systems** into what is typically circulation creates more useable space. The north storage wall acts as an insulated **buffer** to the livable spaces, reducing heat loss along the north exposure. A multi-purpose space, separated from the main bedrooms, provides a flexible space for changing family needs and storage space near the garage. The house is constructed on a **generous 5' crawl space**, adding **long-term storage**.

The **KITCHEN** is designed as an activity center with light entering from east and west. It functions as a "hinge" **7** to create a **separation of living zones** between the north and south wings. The north wing serves the more service-oriented functions of the house such as the garage and laundry room, while the south wing contains the living spaces. The kitchen is thoughtfully located with **access to the garage, outdoor patio space, and living room**.

A **COURTYARD** with **privacy from the street**, offers an area for outdoor **8** dining, children's recreation and social-ization with neighbors. This space incorporates convenient **access from the kitchen** and garage for ease of movement between indoor and outdoor activi-ties. The **defined edges** of the space create an outdoor room that is ideal for barbeques, birthday parties, and other **social gather-ings**. In addition to the west courtyard, a low sitting wall is located along the front of the house to encourage neighborhood socialization.

2003 House

Studio 804

Design/Build Studio
University of Kansas
Lawrence, Kansas

The design/build studio has deviated from our local Habitat for Humanity's typical three-bedroom, one-car garage floor plan in the following ways:

The plan is hinged around the kitchen, creating two wings, north and south. This narrows the depth of the bays to allow more natural daylight to enter the building. The north wing, containing the garage, serves as a buffer to the cold north winds, protecting the living spaces in the south wing. The south facade of the north wing is glazed to passively heat the garage slab for energy efficiency.

The multi-purpose space in the north wing addresses changing family needs. Possible functions include: teenager's bedroom, grandparent's room, nurse/caretaker's room, office and/or shop. This space is separated from the main living area to offer hierarchy of public and private living zones in the house.

The kitchen is designed as an activity center with light from the east and west, rather than an interior corridor with no windows to the outside.

The garage is minimized with access from the rear, leaving the front of the house to respond to the neighborhood, in lieu of the car. Less emphasis is placed on the garage for "curb appeal," and instead, focus is aimed at neighborhood socialization.

The design is compliant with ADA regulations for handicapped accessibility. Careful attention is given to bathroom turnarounds, ramps, and door openings. The garage is designed to enable a handicapped vehicle to meet loading and unloading needs.

The outdoor courtyard space is designed with privacy from the street and easy access from the kitchen to provide an enjoyable area for engaging the homes' exterior.

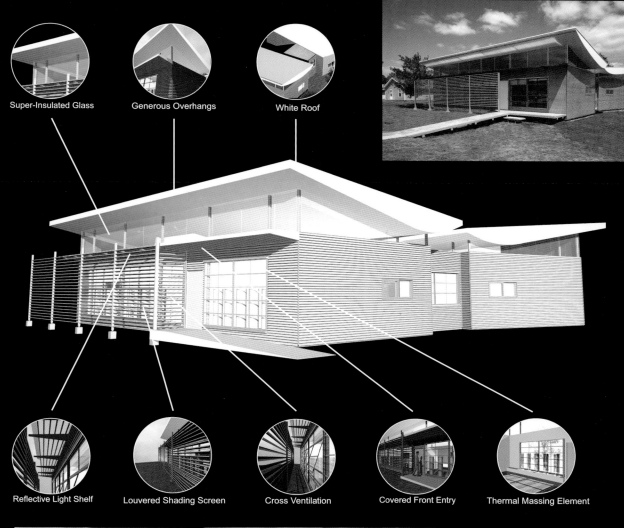

Super-Insulated Glass

Generous Overhangs

White Roof

Reflective Light Shelf

Louvered Shading Screen

Cross Ventilation

Covered Front Entry

Thermal Massing Element

Design/Build Studio

The design/build studio is a **not-for-profit organization** that operates 5 months of the year by 19 architecture students with the leadership of two professors. Students participate in an intensive design/build process each spring that results in a house that is sold to a low-income family. Students work in collaboration with **Tenants to Homeowners**, a local not-for-profit organization, that acts as the client and financial supporter for the construction of the house. The design/build program offers students the opportunity to work with **real clients, neighborhood associations, limited budgets and local building codes**, while establishing a **community-university partnership**. The studio incorporates **innovative design, ADA accessibility, and sustainability** in a house that is sold to a qualified buyer. This is the fifth house to be designed and built by the

Energy Efficiency

The design/build studio operates with the understanding that affordable design is not limited to initial construction costs. The house responds to these issues by using **passive solar design** as a means of decreasing energy consumption to reduce energy bills. Sufficient **insulation** in the ceiling, walls, crawlspace, and clerestory helps to keep energy costs down. Super-insulated glass is used in the clerestory windows to reduce thermal loss through the glazing. A **white single-ply membrane roof** reflects sunlight to minimize summer heat gain. Natural daylighting is maximized throughout the house through the use of highly **reflective interior materials**, reducing electricity costs. Higher efficiency mechanical, electrical, and plumbing systems, such as compact fluorescent lighting and low-flow toilets, ensure lower utility cost for the occu-

Sustainability

The design/build studio strives to achieve environmentally responsible design by incorporating **regional, recycled, recyclable, and salvaged materials** whenever possible. High fly ash content concrete, gravel recycled from crushed concrete, and recycled content insulation and gypsum are used as a means of reducing landfill waste. Industrial steel windows were salvaged from an area building slated for demolition. Corrugated steel siding is used on the exterior of the house as a low-maintenance, **recyclable material**. To avoid destruction of large timbers, laminated veneer lumber is used for roof framing. Recycling and efforts to **minimize waste** occur in the construction process as well. Concrete formwork is dismantled and reused as sub-flooring and framing material. Site waste, such as wood scraps, nails and metal, are all recycled at the

Community

The design/build studio promotes **public conversation and awareness** regarding residential architecture, accessibility, sustainability and the impact of quality design on local residents and their community. Local and national newspapers, television programs and magazines publicize the work of the studio, generating public conversation regarding the **future of affordable housing**. The design/build studio has been featured in the local **Accessible Home Tour, the Earth Day Tour** and area elementary and secondary **educational tours**. Each year, the studio helps to educate local residents and children about accessibility, sustainable practices and recycled materials that can be used in affordable residential design. The design/build studio acts as a **model of quality affordable design** for the local and regional

Accessibility

The design/build studio works to make environments that are **accessible to everyone**, not only financially but also physically. Departing from the local Habitat for Humanity's "visitable" plan, the design/build studio creates a **fully ADA accessible** design. Care is taken to ensure that ramps, turnarounds, fixtures, and door widths fully comply with ADA regulations for handicapped accessibility. Designing with accessibility in mind, the design/build studio ensures that the home will continue to meet the needs of its occupants over time. The house's **multi-purpose room** in the north wing accommodates live-in **nursing or caretaking staff**. It is separated from the main bedrooms to ensure privacy for both the occupants and staff.

Hand-Insulated Pop

Alexander Levi, Augusto Morpurgo, Amanda Schachter
aandacht loop/Morpurgo Architects (ALMA)
Ho-Ho-Kus, New Jersey

The quilt-wall gives the compressed insulation-cavity of an everyday Habitat house facade over to the home-owner as a newfound province of self-expression, in bursts of quilted color throughout the day and night, like an ongoing Independence-Day weekend, Halloween, Christmas, or Kwanzaa. The language of the store window, the highway billboard, and the lawn-jockey all come together to form a new abstract, artful expression of the home-artist, the folk-artist, the truly communicative neighbor. An evening stroll after dinner, to visit a friend's house, walk the dog, or throw out the garbage, allows one to behold home-made and home-exhibited works of art in the salon or picture gallery of the suburban residential street.

The detached single-family home thus reattaches itself to the life of the street. Made from natural wool scraps, the quilt wall is fashioned by each home owner, and can be changed or modified when desired. Hung as insulation between translucent interior panels and translucent plastic siding, the home bathes the sidewalk in warm colors throughout the evening. Lights turned on inside the home, in the living room, dining area, and kitchen cause the home-made quilt-wall to glow from within the otherwise everyday home wall. Low-consumption compact fluorescent tubes can be turned on at night on both sides of the colorful quilt-wall, giving off the embracing warmth of hung tapestry from both outside along the street and inside in the common living areas of each home.

The front façade continues over the soffit and extends seamlessly to the front roof, hovering over the front living areas of the habitat home. This new roof area is surfaced with thin-film photovoltaic cells that form a skylight and cathedral ceiling over the living and dining areas of the home. The glowing quilt-wall can thus be enjoyed in the high-ceiling, sky-lit spaces, and the thin-film, random-silicon-etched glass of the skylight-roof can provide a filtered, clerestory light as well as electricity at least for the wall's lighting needs, as well as for heating, hot water, and appliances. The PV solar panels are installed by the occupants themselves, giving them a new skill they can implement in other houses in the neighborhood.

In the fifties, the Carolina-raised Jasper Johns, through his works of "Hand-Painted Pop," introduced everyday, assumed symbols of America into the realm of art, bringing these over-internalized, no-longer-seen symbols back into plain sight, so that they might again be fully appreciated and scrutinized. In the Hand-Insulated Pop of the quilt-wall, each homeowner can reintroduce self-expression, communication, display, aesthetic beauty, hobby, and artful endeavor to the neighborhood, all within the normal wall of the home.

Legend

1. recycled translucent plastic siding
2. double layer reused bubble-wrap
3. recycled aluminum Z-channels
4. wool shred patchwork quilt
5. recycled translucent plastic panels
6. aluminum tensor to hold quilt
7. compact fluorescent tube
8. Thin-Film photovoltaic array
   acting as 'yankee gutter' and skylight
9. double-thick angel-hair insulation in skylight
10. neoprene gasket or sealant
11. recycled aluminum furring strips
12. stud wall (typical, Habitat For Humanity)
13. rigid insulation (typ. HFH)
14. siding (typ. HFH)
15. gypsum board (typ. HFH)
16. PVC double-hung window (typ. HFH)

Section C
Constructive Wall Section

shaded area signifies alteration to typical HFH house for facade and/or photovoltaic skylight

lower floor plan

wall detail

section c

section a

section b

front elevation

plan

section b

front elevation

Legend

1. recycled translucent plastic siding
2. double layer reused bubble-wrap
3. recycled aluminum Z-channels
4. wool shred patchwork quilt
5. recycled translucent plastic panels
6. aluminum tensor to hold quilt
7. compact fluorescent tube
8. Thin-Film photovoltaic array
   acting as 'yankee gutter' and skylight
9. double-thick angel-hair insulation in skylight
10. neoprene gasket or sealant
11. recycled aluminum furring strips
12. stud wall (typical, Habitat For Humanity)
13. rigid insulation (typ. HFH)
14. siding (typ. HFH)
15. gypsum board (typ. HFH)
16. PVC double-hung window (typ. HFH)

Habitat for Humanity (HFH) 3 Bedroom House

Habitat for Humanity (HFH) 4 Bedroom House

wall detail

VW House / Prefab Modular

Peter Strzebniok, Matthias Troitzsch
NOTTOSCALE
San Francisco, California

Concept: The "VW House" is a modular, prefabricated housing system that incorporates basic production principles from the automobile industry into architecture, providing flexible and affordable housing solutions for different requirements and preferences.

Building: All major components of the "VW House" are prefabricated at the factory. The main difference to the automobile production is, that the house itself is assembled at its final location, allowing the building to respond directly to site and owner specifications. The core of the "VW House" is a pre-fabricated and pre-assembled structural steel chassis that measures 16' x 48' x 10'. The building chassis is made of steel members with predrilled holes that all other building elements attach to. Structurally the chassis is a pre-engineered moment-frame that can be stacked or combined with each other in any possible way.

Floor Plan: The basic unit for the "VW House" measures 768 sf and accommodates two bedrooms, a full bath, an open kitchen, a living area and a storage closet as well as a space for a half bathroom that could also serve as storage space. The base unit can easily grow by combining two units with each other or by adding specific "accessories", modular structures that attach to the main chassis providing additional space if more bedrooms or other functional areas are desired. The sleeping area is subdivided by moveable storage elements that allow the bedroom to be used as one large space or to subdivide it into two bedrooms if needed. The utility block separates the living area from the sleeping area, separating the more intimate spaces without separating the space visually. The open kitchen faces the living area and provides enough space for a small couch, a dining table and a breakfast/kitchen counter. A large porch provides a transition zone from the private to the public realm, which also serves as an extension of the house during the hot summer months.

Ecology/Sustainability

Recognizing the limited nature of natural resources, the VW House is designed to minimize its impact on its location and also to use as little energy and as many recycled materials as possible. The raised chassis provides a crawlspace and eliminates the need for large foundations that seal and damage the land where it is built upon. The building's modular prefabrication process limits the amount of waste common to typical suburban-type developments while providing a quality control standard for the fabrication and construction phase of the building process. The wall panels are preferably manufactured out of recycled or reclaimed materials and already include the wall insulation, ensuring a fast, cheap and energy efficient construction.

Floor Plan / Elevations

Metal Panels

Wood Panels

Plastic Panels

Site Adaptations

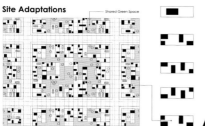

Shared Green Space

Plan Diagram

A

The construction cost is estimated to be at ~ 50.000$, including the steel chassis with foundations, exterior panels with glazing, stud walls w/ gypsum board and paint grade plywood storage units.

Components / Bldg. Parts

1. Steel Frame 16'-0" w x 48'-0" l x 10'-0" h Pre-Assembled and Pre-Finished w/ Pre-Drilled Holes @ 6" o.c. for easy attachment of Panels and other Building Elements.
2. 2'-0" Panel w/ Integrated Insulation
3. 4'-0" Panel w/ Integrated Insulation
4. 6'-0" Panel w/ Integrated Insulation
5. 2'-0" Window Element w/ Aluminum Frame
6. 4'-0" Window Element w/ Aluminum Frame
7. 6'-0" Window Element w/ Aluminum Frame
8. "Punched Hole" Window Element
9. "Panoramic" Window Element
10. Operable Skylight / Ventilation Louver
11. Roof Assembly
12. Floor Assembly
13. Wood Deck w/ Steel Structure and Guardrails
14. Sunshading / Weather Protection
15. Cast in Place Foundations - According to Site and Local Code Requirements
16. Tube Steel Columns w/ Attachment Plate for Building Chassis
17. Utility Block / Plug-In Station
18. Stairs

Site + Community: Single standing developments, re-densification of existing neighborhoods or a variety of more urban, denser environments can easily be created by arranging units in a multitude of ways. The proposed new housing configuration uses a fictional site, arranging different building configurations in a way that creates a variety of spaces with different densities. The different housing types; single-standing, duplex, stacked, courtyard-house, and others, emphasize spatial and social diversity, enhancing the creation of community within the development.

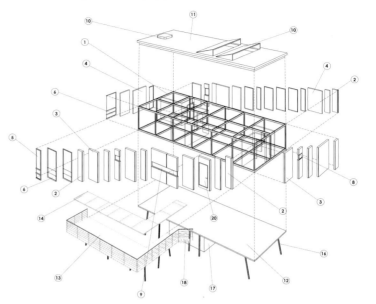

Conception: Choice of Components

Fabrication: Cost Reduction Through Mass Production

Delivery: Speed and Flexibility

Assembly: Ease & Speed of Construction

The assembled and pre-finished chassis is trucked to the site as one unit. Once at the site, the chassis gets mounted onto site-specific columns on spread footings. The floor and roof assembly as well as the exterior wall panels and other interior building units are then attached to the frame. The prefabricated wall panels come in three different widths that are based on a 2'-0" building module. The panels can be fabricated in a variety of different materials, colors and textures, allowing for easy customization. The fenestration is also based on this modular system and can easily be adjusted to match personal preferences or climatic and site specific conditions. All other building units such as the kitchen and the bathroom are based on the same 2'-0" building module and can be arranged within the building chassis to form a variety of different spatial configurations. As the panels and other building elements are not permanently attached, they can easily be exchanged at a later time, allowing for the building to change and evolve over time, responding to the changing needs of the owners. This allows the building to adapt to changing family structures, acknowledging the changing structures of families in our current society.

Free Standing Unit

Truss Design

Base Module

Tricia Stuth, Ted Shelton
Cambridge, England

SAMENESS

The trouble with prototypes is they produce sameness. This seems obvious enough and is perhaps not damning in its own right. Yet, one of the hallmarks of good architecture is its specificity - how well it addresses the particular client, site, climate, and program. In this conflict the dream of a well designed home made affordable through mass production is confronted with its own mutually exclusive ambitions. This is why what is offered here is not a single design, but a system - one that retains the affordability and convenience of a prototype while remaining open-ended for adaptation to the specifics of each situation.

SHOTGUN

This system builds on the regional and historical precedent of the shotgun house. At one time, the shotgun provided a model of an inexpensive and climatically responsive home. Its compactness made it easily constructible with available technology while allowing for cross-ventilation in every room. Its rooms were undelineated, providing flexibility of use. Our solution retains many of the advantages of the shotgun while eliminating many of its shortcomings such as circulation difficulties and limited site responsiveness.

CLIMATIC SPECIFIC RESPONSE

In the Southeast, comfort can be passively achieved 90% of the time with a well-insulated envelope, provided solar gain is managed and natural cross-ventilation is developed. The module is sited so the wall of storage and minimal glazing faces north, reducing heat loss and allowing expansions to the south. These southern expansions are designed to admit sun in winter and exclude sun in summer through manipulation of building form, roofs, cladding and orientation. Natural ventilation is induced by the proportions of the module and the organization of openings and circulation.

BASE MODULE

The key to our approach is the base module. This compact unit contains the kitchen, bathroom, and three rooms for the house and includes all necessary mechanical, electrical, and plumbing work. Dimensions permit the base unit to be manufactured off-site and delivered at the beginning of construction, allowing the work of tradespeople to serve as a foundation for the subsequent efforts of the volunteers. Alternately, the base module can be built from scratch each time - still serving as an armature on which the design of the house is based.

ADAPTATION

Using the base module as an efficient and flexible framework, volunteer architects or supervised architecture students, in the spirit of Auburn's Rural Studio, can then design an expansion that addresses the specific concerns of each client and site. These include topography, solar orientation, client needs and expression, and neighborhood patterns and densities, among other issues. The system's inherent flexibility provides opportunities to use donated building materials and to adjust the size and phasing of the extension for dynamic family and economic conditions. Over time, a catalogue of adaptations will accrue and provide a reference book for future projects.

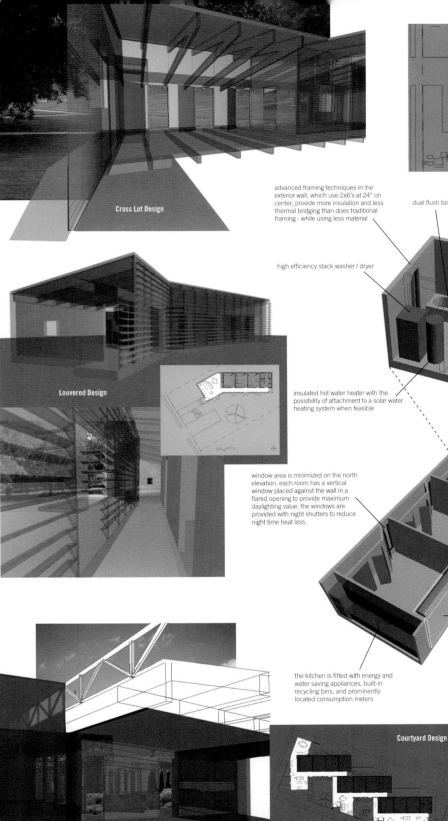

Cross Lot Design

Louvered Design

advanced framing techniques in the exterior wall, which use 2x6's at 24" on center, provide more insulation and less thermal bridging than does traditional framing - while using less material

high efficiency stack washer / dryer

dual flush toilet

low flow faucets at all locations

high efficiency furnace with heat recovery - to be replaced with a combined heat and power unit in future projects as the technology becomes economically accessible in the next few years

insulated hot water heater with the possibility of attachment to a solar water heating system when feasible

window area is minimized on the north elevation. each room has a vertical window placed against the wall in a flared opening to provide maximum daylighting value. the windows are provided with night shutters to reduce night time heat loss.

heating is efficiently distributed in a straight run, minimizing friction in the system and allowing reduced fan energy. central duct supplies both the module rooms to one side and additive room(s) to the other side

the southern wall of the module is clad in 2" of high density wall board, providing thermal mass to even out the extremes of internal temperature

the kitchen is fitted with energy and water saving appliances, built-in recycling bins, and prominently located consumption meters

Courtyard Design

Private Life in the Public Realm

Ben Nicholson

Public housing has always held a bittersweet place in the subconscious of the west. The equivalent of the minimum wage, public housing is the threshold beneath which our societal conscience is not prepared to go. But how high can we afford for that threshold to be? How much are we prepared to do for others?

The benefits of public housing are not just for its residents. We all benefit from living in a society that takes care of its own. Our collective conscience recoils at walking past the homeless and the suffering. But what happens if our charitable instincts outstrip our means? At that point there is a rending of moral fiber. We find ourselves measuring our sense of guilt about the plight of the homeless against our own sense of entitlement for what we have earned. Narrowing the gap between what we would *like* to give the homeless and what we are *willing* to give would benefit both society at large and the residents of the public housing that society provides. But narrowing this gap requires us to think about public housing in creative new ways.

Of the Public

Imagine if a brand new Department of Housing and Social Welfare were established and tasked with solving the unruly problem of matching social conscience with what we are actually capable of paying for.

A committee is formed to probe the issue, and the president attends the opening meeting. Listening to the discussion of the assembled committee, the president remembers a line from the great Texan singer Hank Williams: "A house without love is not a home." Establishing this line as the departmental mission statement, the president charges the new department with building houses filled with love so that everybody can have a homey experience.

The team gets to work immediately. Headquartered in the Disney town of Celebration, researchers fan out across urban and rural landscapes looking for love. They try the obvious first. Surely love will abound in happy, gated subdivisions filled with bright-eyed McMansions. But the team is disappointed. Intimidated by the sheer size of their houses and exhausted by the long walks from one part of the house to the other, the inhabitants of these repositories of emptiness rattle about aimlessly. The opulent marble whirlpools and professionally equipped kitchens barely get used; the occupants essentially camp out in electrified La-Z-Boy recliners in the den, linked to one or two bar stools pitched around the microwave in the kitchen. The cathedral-ceilinged formal rooms with their satin-covered loveseats, which looked so enticing in the sales brochures, are as sterile and uninviting as a morgue.

Deciding to explore extremes, the team visits an encampment of the "homeless" under a freeway bridge, and are startled to find that this encampment comes much closer to fitting the president's profile than the McMansion did. Apart from hunger, fratricidal squabbles, and fights over available climatic resources (common to even the wealthiest domicile, but on a different scale), here everything is in order. The shopping cart used for all transportation needs is adjacent to the bed; cooking equipment is a part of the burning-pallet heating system; and a change of venue is provided periodically by the police, who occasionally visit the encampment and smash up everything, which enables the sort of drastic remodeling that the suburbanites crave and claim never to be able to afford.

Reaching the obvious conclusion, the team dutifully prepares its report and slaps it onto desk in the Oval Office. The President scans the diagrams and accompanying photographic records and raises his eyebrows. "The people have spoken," he declares to the circle of trembling peons. "And if that's what people want, then you can darn well give it to 'em!"

The department wheels out new housing prototypes, each designed to be a domain that mediates between day and night, activity and rest, the essential requisites of living, plus a little more. Hundreds of thousands of carefully crafted micro-mobile homes are built, soon dubbed M&M's, which have all the essentials of living. M&M's come in

different sizes: For the homeless and for individuals on the go who require zero fixity, there is the purpose-built shopping-cart home. For people who appreciate the benefits of para-fixity, the team develops an M&M caravan, whose size is one third of the square footage of the standard mobile home. Fixed-in-place 4' x 4'

MMX-1
The MMX-1 conceptual prototype for the Micro Mobile Home Initiative.

x 8' sleeping M&M's, modeled on the highly successful Japanese Capsule Hotels for travelers, are constructed for those who would like something bolted down to earth. The tiny residences become popular with the homeless as well as with travelers on a tight budget. Thus the existing model of the single-room-occupancy residence, measuring 7 feet by 10 feet, is supplemented by something much more modest, and every citizen has the opportunity to get a good night's rest in a safe, private, and warm environment.

Cities across the country build oases in which residents can park these mobile domains for a nominal charge. The municipality provides cleaning, eating, clothing, health, and storage facilities, which any socially minded culture would be happy to provide. Security and maintenance workers who once had to patrol the streets to identify and destroy the homeless encampments are now employed as gardeners, and are charged with establishing a unique landscape for each of the home oases. The unique character of the gardens gives each oasis an individual quality, which draws quite different patrons. With the system in place, the formerly homeless and Z Generation find themselves rubbing shoulders, one constituency having picked up their M&M's at the airport, and the other at a Center for Health and Human Services.

For families and groups of persons who wish to live in the same space, a larger square footage is made available, but once again the appointments are modest, efficient, and very well maintained. The base concept is for the domestic realms to be straightforward and the communal realms to be conversational, interactive, and inviting. The home complexes allocate the lion's share of their budgets to the operation of communal facilities such as washerterias, swimming pools, playgrounds, and communal halls for larger gatherings.

The oases also provide decks and individual garden allotments so that the residents can spend time in neighborly recreation. The individual gardens contribute to the overall feeling that home life inside and outside is one and the same thing. The craft of tending plants is aided and abetted at every opportunity. A member of staff helps residents with gardening questions, and is recognized as being an essential part of everybody's life. In the summer months the tended grass becomes a flexible carpet. In the winter months the sun is brought into the living room to warm and delight.

No prejudice is leveled at the winter sun as inferior to the summer sun; the qualities of both are taken for what they are: life giving.

Of the Private

After the Department of Housing and Social Welfare has concluded the bulk of its work for the public sector, the team moves on to assess the health of housing in the private sector. Research teams examine the patterns of the professional classes and determine that their movements are akin to transitory Bedouin tribepeople, shifting from suburb to suburb in regular succession as work makes itself available across the country. Fleets of slow-moving hybrid-engined U-Hauls and Allied Van Lines, resembling caravans of laden camels, clog the nation's freeway system to shuttle collected possessions from one neck of the woods to the next.

The team finds that the transitory professional classes of America typically live beneath quickly erected piles of 2 by 4's, rock wool, polystyrene foam, and plastic sheathing. These structures are perpetually temperature-controlled by invisible roaring furnaces and cooling systems designed to give the illusion of perpetual summer. Windows are never opened—not even in the transitional seasons of spring and fall. The real nature of American construction techniques becomes evident when the team happens upon a house fire. In the conflagration, the house essentially melts, the burning plastic dripping onto the ground forming puddles of fire, fanned into action by the sheet goods of the chipped lumber industry and held in place by a devil's kitchen of toxic glues.

Examining the land use necessary to support the McMansion syndrome, the team determines that it has crippled vast acreages of farmland around our cities. Taking a cue from European urban-planning models, the Department of Housing and Social Welfare clamps the land around the cities in a restricted green belt in which no new residence or business can be constructed. Pedestrian rights of way crisscross this intermediary landscape, giving access to the idyllic life of farm urban dwellers in a way that dissolves the tyranny of land ownership, reverting back to the American Indian concept of stewardship and not ownership of the land.

Each square foot of existing suburbia is examined carefully for its possibilities. The wanton commandeering of plentiful land, a hangover of the nineteenth-century

Green Belt Cottage
An idyllic rural homestead situated in the green belts of urbanism

expansion west, is brought up fast and hard. The days of property speculation and greed are relegated to myth. Black Infinity SUV's sporting puffy-faced real estate brokers roll to a grinding halt. The What-I-Wanters are forced to confront their slash-and-burn mentality.

In order to conserve energy within the existing stock of McMansions, the Department of Housing and Social Welfare decrees that houses be heated only to the level that Great Grandpa knew—the mid-50°s. To achieve this, the department recommends that residents consider the advantages of point heat. For the Europeans this means a log fire; for the Japanese it means a few pieces of charcoal placed in a brazier supplying heat to the warmed circle of a happily chatting family; and for the new urbanist, it means wearing a woolly hat and sweater.

Tests show that a well-made hat reduces body heat loss by 30 percent, and thus has the potential to reduce heating bills by 30 percent. Each house is fitted with an extensive hat rack, sporting a number of different types of hats for the use of residents and visitors alike. The department begins its exploration of the use of headwear by experimenting with the design of the

American baseball hat, a national headwear equivalent to the Sikh's turban and Muslim's skull cap or head scarf. The baseball cap, whose brim is essentially a veranda to keep the sun out of the wearer's eyes, is converted to be more appropriate for indoor use. Over a period of years the brim's bill gradually shrinks, and eventually the winterized indoor baseball hat has a _" symbolic rim running along its front edge.

Expanding on existing metaphorical language that describes housing attributes in terms of bodily experience (e.g. eye-candy, thumb-candy and taste-treats), the department coins the term "heat treat" to denote a break from wearing a hat or nightcap. A heat treat is an option for a family that wants to splurge. "Shall we go buy something," they ask, "or shall we stay in for a heat treat?" If they opt for the heat treat, they forego a triple scoop of Ben and Jerry's ice cream and turn their home heater up to 78° so that they can trip around the house in tee-shirts, awash in nostalgia for the good old days of apparent plenty and the illusion of perpetual summer.

Practical Solutions

Although prototypes always have the advantage of not having to cope with the messiness of real time politics, it is nevertheless a relief to know that someone is willing to have a go at righting the First World's domain. A consenting cooperative of builders called SIMPARCH is building a home at the Center of Land Use Interpretation in Wendover, Utah. The house is stuck out in the middle of the briny Utah flats, a terrain that has witnessed fifty years of bullets, bombs, and a plethora of nasty chemistry. It is the harshest landscape that imaginable, yet a smidgen of a house is going up that answers the eternal yearning for utopia.

Aided by a cadre of investigator/makers from the Illinois Institute of Technology, SIMPARCH has produced a work that rethinks the home/house combo. Called Clean Livin', the house itself is a 1940s quonset hut converted

Solar Cells
The electric mini-grid, water tower, and house unit of Clean Livin'.

Bomb Quilt
The Bomb Quilt commemorates Wendover's part in Hiroshima.

Water Porter
The children deliver fifty-five gallons of water for domestic consumption by bike powered Water Porter.

into a scorpion-proof plywood checkerboard. Furniture is built out of recycled plywood, hand selected from prime-quality real-estate signage from Chicago. Each plywood sheet touts the glories of opulent marble Jacuzzis and multiplex condo living, the graphic texts making an eerie counterpart to the straightforward life the plywood sheets are now being used to support. Rag carpets are woven from used tee-shirts handed out at corporate picnics. Bedding counterpanes are quilted to record the Little Man/Fat Boy bombing history of the site—the Enola Gay and Bock's Car B-29 Stratofortress bombers departed from Wendover for their boiling milkruns to Hiroshima and Nagasaki in 1945. Clean Livin' addresses every little detail of the techno-topian domestic realm with encounters such as these, and a whole lot more.

In the Clean Livin' house the week starts with a two-mile bike ride to collect fifty-five gallons of water in a human-powered Water Porter vehicle, the whole experience acting as gym replacement therapy. The water from the Water Porter is pumped up into a tower and then gravity fed into Clean Livin's water system. But not everything in Clean Livin' works on leg power. As the sun rises over the horizon, $7,500.00 worth of solar cells crank into action, providing an electrical mini-grid for the household.

Clean Livin' in the House/Home

Upon waking up one morning, make the declaration that from this day forward you pledge to not be possessed by possessions! Once you've made that promise, your life will change for the better. For one thing, you're quite unlikely to find much appeal in a bloated home within which to store all that stuff, for why would anyone want to make a house to conform to the aspirations of indentured suburbia? Your priorities will shift to valuing an existence that bends technology for the betterment of the soul. Your ideal house will make a pact with the strictures of the electrical grid, sewage lines, and gurgling water mains, taking no more than is needed and giving back a surplus.

Making art and creating architecture is a biological need—not an optional luxury for the well-to-do. The body politic will atrophy if it is not nurtured. The new standard created by SECCA's HOME House Project, indexed to the nation's tolerance for providing what it deems a fair and equitable living arrangement for all its citizens, lends verse to the mix. The Clean Livin' project prods our real-time eco-conscience, recalibrating our vision of utopia. Together, the marriage of art & politics and politics & art makes our collective vision of who we are, the median zone within which society ultimately settles. Without initiatives like SECCA's HOME House Project and Clean Livin', the built world would evolve into a gray zone full of practical solutions yet devoid of poetry, and such a zone would be an open-air prison for us all.

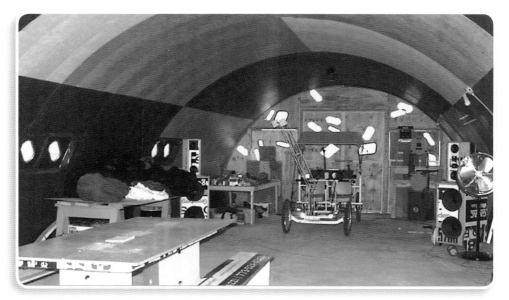

Inside Clean Livin'
Inside the home on the Utah Salt Flats.

Steve Badanes

Excerpts from a conversation with David J. Brown, October 18, 2003

Note: *HOME House Project juror Steve Badanes holds the Howard Wright Endowed Chair at the University of Washington in Seattle, where he leads design/build studios that have focused on community service projects for nonprofit organizations in the Seattle area. Badanes is a founder of Jersey Devil, an architectural firm perpetuating the tradition of medieval craftsmen. The firm is comprised of skilled craftsmen, architects, inventors, and artists "committed to the interdependence of building and design." Jersey Devil architects/builders live on-site during construction of their designs, which are known for energy efficiency and innovative use of materials. Badanes has lectured on Jersey Devil's work at more than 100 universities in the United States, Canada, Mexico, and Europe and has informed many university design/build programs, including Auburn's heralded Rural Studio, founded by Samuel Mockbee and D.K. Ruth.*

On socially-responsive architecture: Jersey Devil was part of the counterculture—the first generation of hippie architects. We were inspired by the space program: If you could put a guy out in space, self-contained, why would we need all of the umbilical cords here on earth? You could build the earthbound equivalent of a space capsule that was off the grid, a building that generated its own energy, grew its own food, and was completely self-sufficient. There were people with the foresight to see that we were running out of resources. …Architects have a great gift. We can design things; we can build things; we can change people's lives with what we make. We can use our skills to make the world better.

Architecture as a profession: Before the 1900's, master builders traveled from town to town and would plan a house and build it from pattern books. With the onset of the industrial revolution in the early 1900's, houses began to be built more efficiently. There were groups of people that set themselves apart as a trade ("architects") and developed an organization that became the American Institute of Architects. In 1909, the AIA ruled that architects could not build. The relationship between hand and mind was severed. It was not until the 1980 recession that decision was reversed.

The size of houses in America: We are building houses that are more efficient, but they are a lot bigger so everything is going to cost a lot more. When a builder builds a house, there's not much incentive to keep the operating cost down—what they want to do is to keep the first cost down. Increasing the amount of square footage that the American family seems to need (which has doubled in one generation) has negated any gains that we have made in efficiency.

The schooling of architects: The profession of architecture has become less satisfying to someone who has just come out of school—you do not draw with a

Hui Du, Yiling Mackay
Gaithersburg, Maryland

pencil anymore. You have to push that bar of soap around all day long and look at a screen, which is a lot less satisfying than working by hand, where each drawing has an individual style. An architectural pencil drawing is an abstraction of a building, and a computer drawing is an abstraction of the pencil drawing, so you're pretty far away from the gut process of making something, and the reasons a lot of us go into this business is to make things.

Water and gasoline: In Europe, gasoline costs 4 or 5 dollars a gallon, but here in the United States gas costs about the same as bottled drinking water. America uses very little domestic oil. We get oil from the Middle East, and we fight wars to keep the shipping lanes open. Then when it gets over here it goes through middlemen and refineries and the price is bumped up at each stop, but when it gets to the pump it's still the same price as drinking water. Now either the guys who supply the drinking water are making an incredible profit, or we are not charging enough for the gasoline. If we were to crank up the price of gasoline, alternative energy and conservation would be more prevalent and our foreign policy might change. It would really help if we paid a little bit more for gasoline and a lot less for military solutions to our energy problems.

LEED ratings: We now have the Leadership in Energy and Environmental Design rating for evaluating the effectiveness of sustainable design. To be a green architect, you need to be LEED certified. I think it has had a positive influence, particularly with government and commercial buildings—buildings that need to make an impression that they are designed the right way.

Green architecture: Buildings use 40 percent of all energy, which does not include the energy embodied in materials and construction. Nuclear energy, oil, and coal represent death and environmental destruction; solar energy, renewables, and recycling represent sustenance and survival. So it's a pretty simple: If you want to contribute to the continuation of the species, you will focus on green architecture, small efficient dwellings, and social responsibility.

PVC and public policy: The truth about PVC has come out: It kills people in the manufacturing process and in the region where it's made, and you can't dispose of it. Why would anyone want to use it? Well, it is not hard to work with, and it lasts for a long time. Why should society care if some guy from Louisiana dies from making it, or all the neighbors do? One problem is the lobbyists for the big corporations—like the Vinyl Institute. It is not a level playing field in terms of government regulations. Each of us has one vote but the guys that make the big contributions have more power when it comes to getting things done. The environment is the main thing that suffers: Although it contributes to our quality of life and our survival on earth, it does not make political contributions, so it keeps getting beaten up.

Government support for alternative energy: Not since President Jimmy Carter and the 1970's oil crisis has there been government support for non-fossil fuels or solar energy. Carter enacted tax credits for solar energy and insulation and energy-saving devices. He put solar collectors on the White House as a symbol. He put environmentalists and concerned scientists in the Department of Energy and declared the "moral equivalent of war" on the energy issue. In addition, people responded. We traded in our big Cadillacs for more energy-efficient cars; we bought wood stoves; we insulated our houses and kept our thermostats low. We didn't flush our toilets every time. When Reagan entered office, he said we could take those solar collectors and burn them in our "nuclear furnaces." He took the collectors off the White House, fired all the environmentalists in the Department of Energy and repealed the tax credits because he was indebted to all the coal, oil, and nuclear industries, which had all contributed heavily to his campaign.

Nuclear energy, oil, and coal represent death and environmental destruction: solar energy, renewables, and recycling represent sustenance and survival.

Basic economics: Economics is how we make decisions in homebuilding. When it becomes too expensive to do things one way, we start to do something else. But we basically do the cheapest thing. When the cheapest thing turns out to be using recycled materials, then we will use them. The cost of disposing our waste is escalating. The construction industry generates an enormous quantity of waste, and it used to be that we could put a giant dumpster at the site and put the contents in a landfill. Nowadays that is expensive, so even a big construction company will get a bid for recycling sheetrock, wood, and metal. Now that it is worth paying a guy to find a place to reuse building materials, wood is recycled into engineered wood products or it goes into industrial arts programs. If recycling costs more, builders are not all that big hearted, they will just throw stuff away. The same goes for fuel. As soon as we start paying the same for gasoline as the rest of the world, we'll have plenty of hybrid cars in this country.

Urban sprawl and the quality of life: I don't think there's anything to celebrate about our quality of life if you are in your car all day long making twenty trips a day from your house to fill the most basic of needs and having to sit in traffic. It seemed like such a great idea in the 40's and 50's: the open road and the freedom of the car and the romance and the rest of it. However, it seems like more of a nightmare now.

Walkable communities: Finland is not a highly populated country; it is as big as California, with only a fraction of the people. But you'll go for 25 or 30 miles of virgin countryside, lakes, and woods and then you'll hit a town. And the town will be packed together. Hardly anybody will have a car. Everybody will have an apartment. It's so cold; why would you want to heat a house? The urban life is something they like. They all have little vacation cabins that they go to in the summertime, but it's the summer and you don't need heat, and you have a month to enjoy it because you have cheap socialized medicine, and you don't have to work so hard to pay for a big house, car, and private health insurance.

Environmentalists: Everybody will talk about being an environmentalist, but they are capitalists at heart. I once invested in a company that made backpacks from the waste stream from the local industries. All the materials were recycled. I thought, people will love to use this; this will work. But people who say they're environmentalists will go in the store and if the recycled backpack costs three dollars more than the other backpack, they won't buy it. If you want to affect some changes in this culture you have to strike at the economy. In thirty or forty years we'll run out of oil no matter who owns it, and when that happens we will be forced to change our ways. However, by that time we will have pretty much fouled up the ozone layer and the Alaskan Natural Wildlife Refuge and much of the rest of the planet.

Mobile homes: A mobile home is the cheapest possible solution for rural sites. But unlike almost any other building, a mobile home doesn't increase in value. It's like a car. The minute you buy it, it starts to decrease in value. It is built flimsily, hard to heat and cool, and it will burn in a second. There is a reason why it does not appreciate in value; there is not much value there to start with. But travel trailers, in particular, have come up with some real innovations in terms of space usage, in terms of prefabrication and mechanical systems, in terms of self-containment. The travel trailer is like a little space ship. Right away it uses less energy, uses less land. A trailer park comes as close to being a little community as we have in rural America — because there are common facilities there.

Alternative materials: When I worked in Africa, I saw housing built with stacked shipping containers with roofs spanning between them. Containers have always provided some sort of storage. I think you can get one on your property quite inexpensively, but the problem is that you have to cut them open (lead paint!) and spend major money and time adapting them to habitation. Still, there are advantages to looking at things that are not typically used for housing—things that are used in industrial or agricultural applications where there are no frills—where things have to be cheap, durable, and more efficient. You need natural ventilation

Maggie Peng, Ada Tolla, Giuseppe Lignano, Guy Zucke
LOT-EK Architecture
New York, New York

in a chicken house or all the chickens will die. So look at how those farm and industrialized buildings are designed: linear, good stack ventilation, etc. In many cases if you have good ones you have plenty of daylight, and workers are more productive working in natural light and ventilated spaces.

Prefab houses: I am designing a small house in North Carolina and the covenants say that if any more than 20 percent of a house is built offsite, they do not have to take it. In other words, they don't want any prefabricated houses—probably because they don't want any trailers. But almost 90 percent of every house is built offsite. What do you call windows, doors, toilets, cabinets, and tile? Construction these days has been simplified by assembling manufactured components. It is possible that maybe the entire house should be manufactured before it comes to the site. So far, this method has not been cheap, but with new technologies, that seems to be changing.

The do-it-yourself industry: In 98 percent of the housing in this country, the people who live in it never have anything to say about what's going to be in their house or how it's built. That is why the do-it-yourself industry is so strong. People visit the home stores because they live in a generic house that was designed for some imaginary family: a husband, a stay-at-home wife, and a couple of kids. And it turns out that most of our families are not like that. We've got single moms;

we've got all kinds of people in housing; same-sex couples. It is a shame that most housing by builders is designed for a market that does not exist anymore so people have to modify it.

On recycling: One of the biggest problems with the manufacturing sector in this country is that manufacturers are not responsible for recycling their own products. We purchase TV's and computers every couple of years, but it is our problem as the consumer to get rid of them when we're done with them. If industry were required to take their products back, they would design them so that they could reuse almost everything in them. Instead of a linear process, you would have created a loop. Recycle.

On Habitat for Humanity: Habitat for Humanity is a great idea. The whole idea of bringing volunteers together and having everybody have a "feel good" experience building a house for somebody who really needs one is great. I can't argue with that. However, at this point Habitat is a very large homebuilder, and for many reasons, their product is not very good. They use a cookie-cutter plan that is similar in every region of the country. In some places there should be a different orientation, different shape of the house—a longer house in the south, where ventilation that is more natural is needed; a tighter one in the north, where you have big heating bills. A house needs to respond to its region, to its climate. And many times, there is a poor choice of materials. A lot of Habitat houses have vinyl siding. There are definite reasons why you should not use vinyl because of the PCBs, the dioxins, and the chemical problems with it. It cannot be recycled, and it causes health problems during its production and destruction. Since the environmental agenda of Habitat is not so great, given the volume of houses they are producing, we may be creating a liability for the future. I mean, are we building slums or are we solving housing problems? The environmental agenda should not be separate from the perceived social agenda. But it seems so far that Habitat is not that interested in the environmental agenda. They should think about what an energy-efficient, affordable house of the future looks like and go ahead and build prototypes instead of cranking out boxes that are unresponsive in terms of the region, the climate, and in a sense the client.

Selected Images from

The HOME House Project Submissions

Process 2
Ryan Spruston/Sean Anlquist
San Francisco, CA

Square Feet Studio
John Bencich, Mike Boland, Mark Blair
Atlanta, GA

Borden Partnership
Gail Peter Borden
Raleigh, NC

Todd Boyd
Somerville, MA

David D. Brown, Rebecca Sharkey,
Sam Zimmerman-Bergman,
Sharon Gallant, Tim Stauffer
Albany, CA

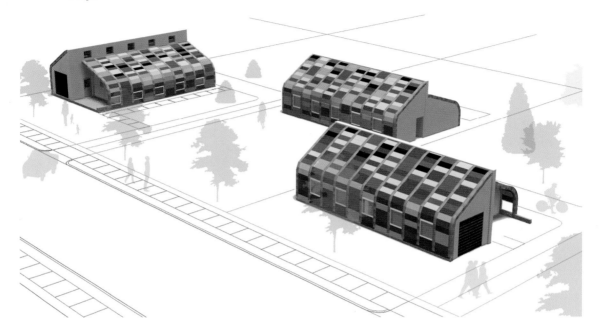

Rob Bradford, Maria Perez Gensler
Houston, TX

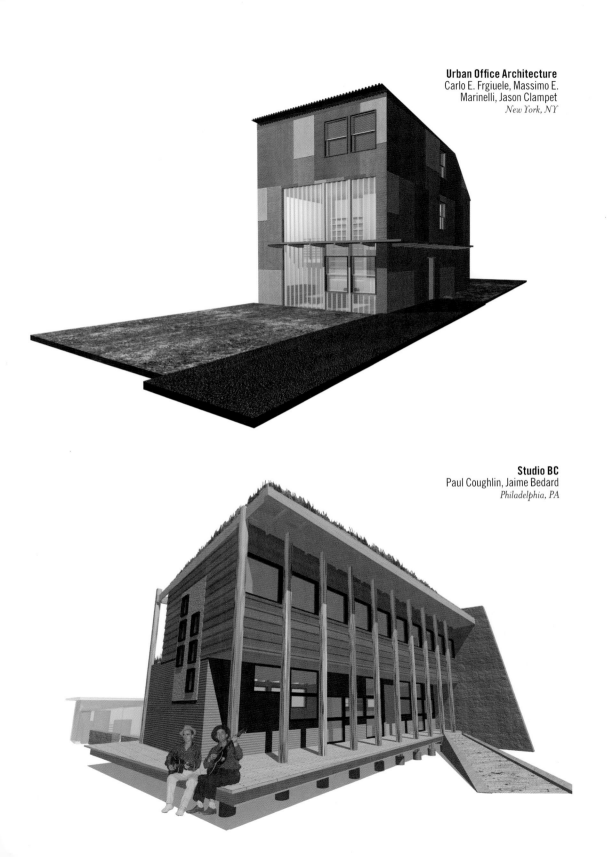

Urban Office Architecture
Carlo E. Frgiuele, Massimo E.
Marinelli, Jason Clampet
New York, NY

Studio BC
Paul Coughlin, Jaime Bedard
Philadelphia, PA

Bill Edgerton
Charlottesville, VA

Engs Architects
Ned Engs
Los Angeles, CA

Gabriel Feld
Cambridge, MA

DSH
Eric Haas, Chava Danielson, Michael Aquino
Los Angeles, CA

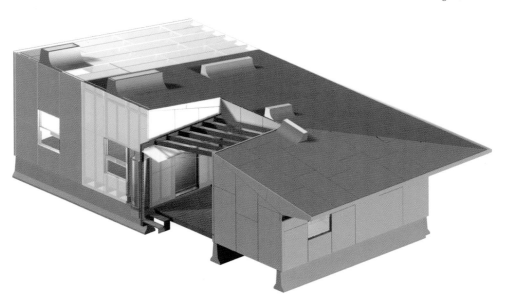

David M. Harmon
Denver, CO

Henriquez Partners Architects
Sandy Hirshen, Rui Nunes
Vancouver, Canada

Christopher Hood
Boxborough, MA

Robert Humble Architects
Robert Humble, Jonathan Barriger
Seattle, WA

Dan Vos Construction Co.
Bruce Medendorp
Ada, MI

Project Quest
Darren M. Kelly
Columbus, OH

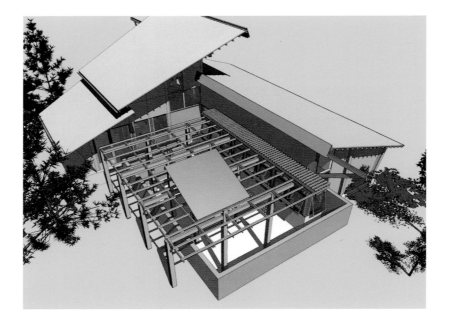

Motonobu Kurokawa
New York, NY

Nam hoon Kim
Cambridge, MA

Ilg Luis Pathangey & Soenksen Design
Lira Luis, Chris LLg, Navin Pathangay, Steve Soenksen
Phoenix, AZ

Green Sky Design
Eric McDaniel
Portland, OR

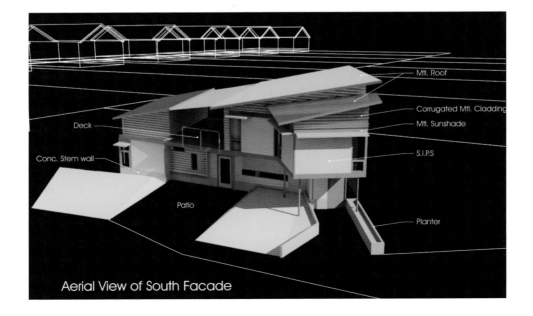

Mtl. Roof

Corrugated Mtl. Cladding

Deck — Mtl. Sunshade

Conc. Stem wall — S.I.P.S

Patio

Planter

Aerial View of South Facade

Yost Grube Hall Architecture
Paul Mckean
Portland, OR

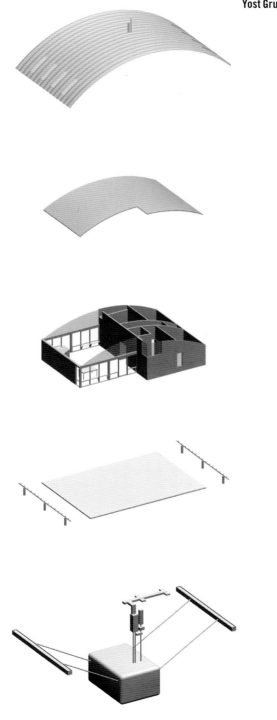

Edward Mitchell
New Haven, CT

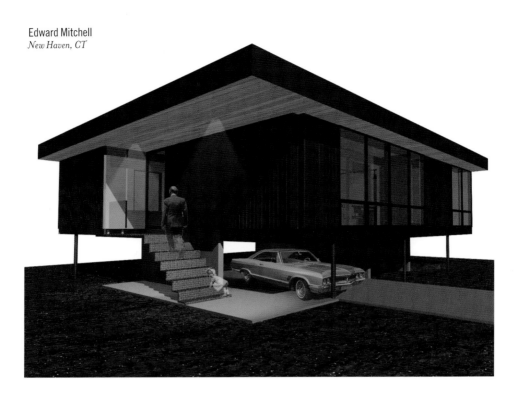

Oliver Centanni
Vancouver, Canada

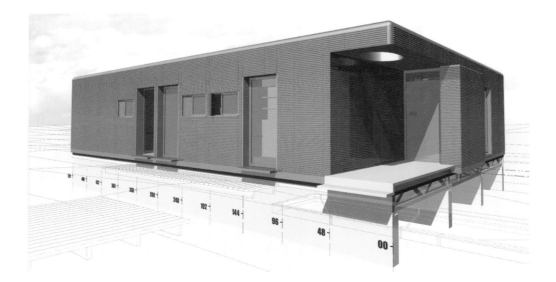

Radonjic & Partners
Miljan Radonjic, Aleksander Jovanovic
Pancevo, SERBIA & MONTENEGRO

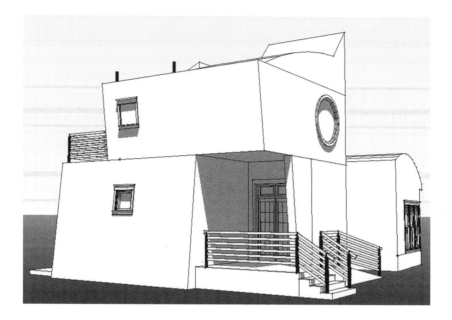

Juan C. Ricardes
Tampa, FL

Jonah Ritter
Minneapolis, MN

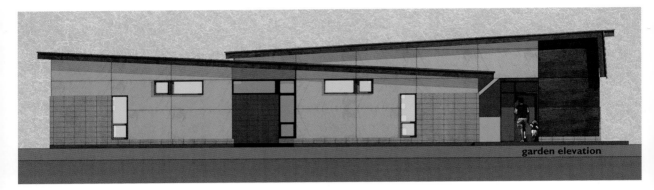

garden elevation

Schwartz Architects
W. Douglas Romines
New York, NY

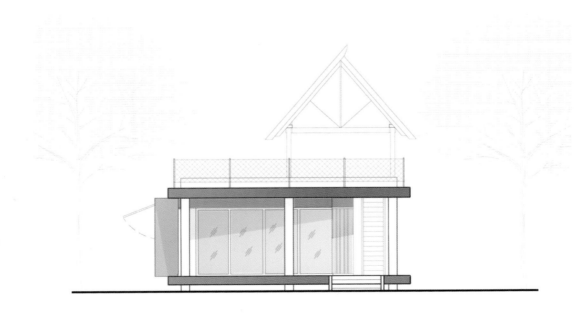

Pulse3am
George Roushakes
New York, NY

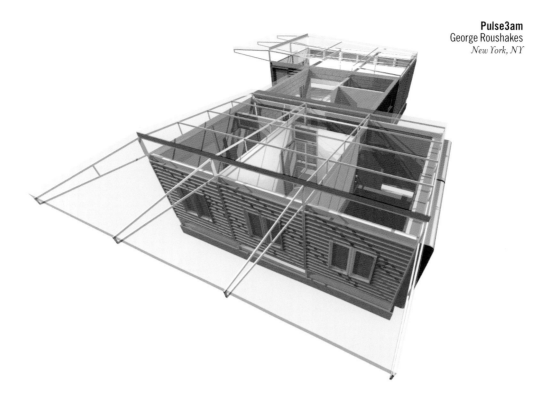

Marmol Radziner & Associates
Nicole Cannon, Huay Wee
Los Angeles, CA

Chad Smith
San Francisco, CA

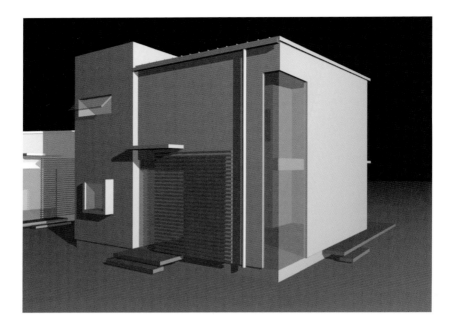

Gerich / Spencer
Benjamin R. Spencer
Charlottesville, VA

Sleeve
Marc Swackhamer (School of Architecture & Interior Design,
University of Cincinnati,) and Blair Satterfield (Bricker & Canaday
Architects & Rice University - Houston) with consultants, Robert
Burnham (University of Cincinnati) and Cory Satterfield (Flad and
Associates, Madison)
Cincinnati, OH

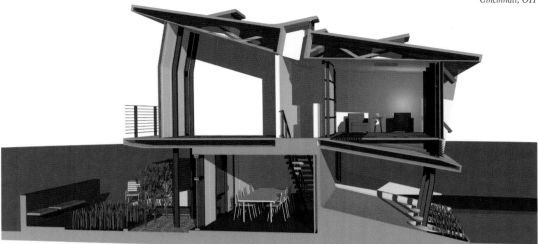

Lisa Tidler
Knowlton School of Architecture, Ohio State University
Columbus, OH

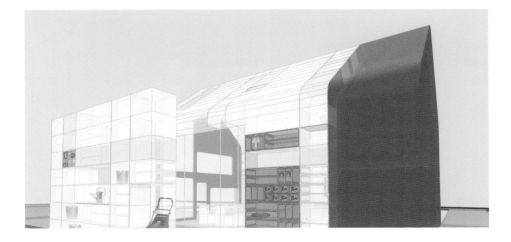

Robert Ventura
Richmond, VA

CCS Architecture
Cass Calder Smith, Aaron Maret
San Francisco, CA

Cerrone and Wagstaff Architects
Mary Cerrone, Kevin Wagstaff
Pittsburgh, PA

Allan Wexler
New York, NY

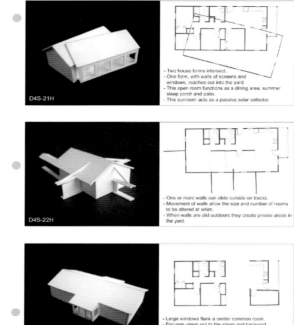

D4S-21H
- Two house forms intersect.
- One form, with walls of screens and windows, reaches out into the yard.
- This open room functions as a dining area, summer sleep porch and patio.
- This sunroom acts as a passive solar collector.

D4S-22H
- One or more walls can slide outside on tracks.
- Movement of walls allow the size and number of rooms to be altered at whim.
- When walls are slid outdoors they create private areas in the yard.

D4S-23H
- Large windows flank a center common room.
- Focuses views out to the street and backyard.
- Family spaces recieve both morning and afternoon light.
- Common room extends into a sunroom and entry porch.

page 3

Shinya Yamada, Juan Calaf,
Peter Aeschbacher
Los Angeles, CA

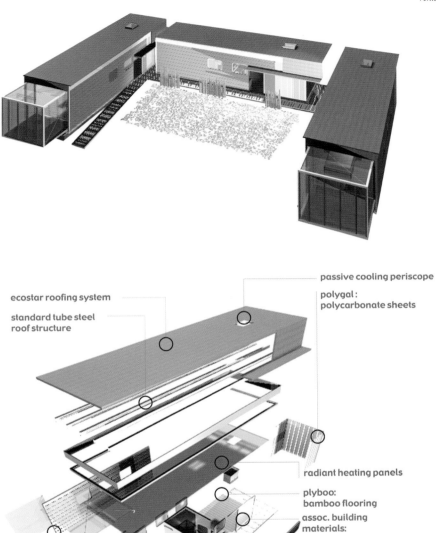

passive cooling periscope

ecostar roofing system

polygal :
polycarbonate sheets

standard tube steel
roof structure

radiant heating panels

plyboo:
bamboo flooring

assoc. building
materials:
aluminum doors

homasote:
wall finish

A-1 flooring:
rubber flooring

metal siding

advanced foam plastics:
structural insulated wall panels

milgard:
aluminum windows

aurora:
steel framework

About the Authors

Michael Sorkin is the principal of the Michael Sorkin Studio in New York City, a design practice devoted to both practical and theoretical projects at all scales with a special interest in the city. Recent projects include masterplanning in Hamburg and Schwerin, Germany, planning for a Palestinian capital in East Jerusalem, campus planning at the University of Chicago, and studies of the Manhattan waterfront and Arverne, Queens. The studio is the recipient of a variety of awards, including three I.D. Awards and a Progressive Architecture Award. Sorkin is the Director of the Graduate Urban Design Program at the City College of New York. From 1993 to 2000 he was Professor of Urbanism and Director of the Institute of Urbanism at the Academy of Fine Arts in Vienna. Previously, Sorkin has been professor at numerous schools of architecture including Cooper Union (for ten years), Columbia, Yale (holding both Davenport and Bishop Chairs), Harvard, Cornell (Gensler Chair), Nebraska (Hyde Chair), Illinois, Pennsylvania, Texas, and Minnesota. Sorkin lectures widely and is the author of many articles in a wide range of both professional and general publications and is currently contributing editor at *Architectural Record* and *Metropolis*. For ten years, he was the architecture critic of *The Village Voice*. His books include *Variations on A Theme Park, Exquisite Corpse, Local Code, Giving Ground* (edited with Joan Copjec), *Wiggle,* a monograph of the studio's work, *Some Assembly Required,* and *Other Plan.*, Forthcoming are *Weed, AZ., The Next Jerusalem, Work On The City,* and *After The Trade Center* (edited with Sharon Zukin). Sorkin was born in Washington, D.C. and received his architectural training at Harvard and MIT.

Ben Nicholson studied architecture at the Architecture Association in London and Cooper Union, and received a Master of Architecture from Cranbrook Academy in 1982. He is a Studio Professor of Architecture at the Illinois Institute of Technology, Chicago, where he has lived for the past 12 years. His publications include *The Appliance House,* 1990, and a CD-Rom *Ben Nicholson: Thinking the Unthinkable House,* 1997, that includes *The Loaf House project.* His website is www.bennicholson.com. Currently he is writing a book about the arrangement of information and the hidden geometric pavements in Michelangelo's Laurentian Library. He has also advised on a documentary film about the B-52 Stratofortress Bomber. He has exhibited at The Canadian Center of Architecture, The Renaissance Society, The Cartier Foundation, the Henie Onstat Museum, Oslo, and the Whitney Museum of American Art at Altria. He has received grants from the Chicago Institute for Architecture & Urbanism and The Graham Foundation.

David J. Brown received a BFA at Old Dominion University and a MFA from Virginia Commonwealth University. He is currently the Senior Curator and *HOME House Project* Director at the Southeastern Center for Contemporary Art (SECCA), Winston-Salem,

North Carolina. Before joining the staff at SECCA in 1999, Brown was the Curator at the Contemporary Arts Center, Cincinnati (96-99), and the Director of Exhibitions at the Maryland Institute, College of Art, Baltimore, Maryland (89-96). Brown served on the Board of Directors at the Washington Project for the Arts in Washington, DC from (85-90). He has curated, organized, and toured more than sixty exhibitions and community-based projects including *The HOME House Project, the future of affordable housing; Tongues on Fire: Visions and Ecstasy with Lesley Dill; David Byrne: What Is It?, Yoko Ono: En Trance; Beyond Glory: Re-Presenting Terrorism; Theater of Excess: An Installation by David Mach; Roy Lichtenstein: Man Hit by the 21st Century;* and many others. Besides producing numerous exhibition catalogs, Brown teamed with Dr. Robert Merrill to publish the book: *Violent Persuasions: The Politics and Imagery of Terrorism* (1993), Bay Press, Seattle, WA.

Steve Badanes attended Wesleyan University for undergraduate studies and Princeton University, where he received his Master of Architecture degree. He has received grants from the National Endowment for the Arts and the Graham Foundation for Advanced Studies in the Fine Arts, as well as a Fellowship from the Association of Collegiate Schools of Architecture. He has conducted design/build workshops at the University of Technology in Helsinki, Finland, the University of Oregon, the University of Washington, the University of Miami, Ball State University, the University of California at San Diego, Florida A&M University, Miami University in Ohio North Dakota State University, and the University of Wisconsin.

As a practicing architect, his commissions have included private homes, schools, public structures, and the winning entry, *The Fremont Troll* in the *Hall of Giants* 1990 Competition in Seattle, Washington. Badanes is a founder of Jersey Devil, an architectural firm perpetuating the tradition of medieval craftsmen. The firm is comprised of skilled craftsmen, architects, inventors, and artists "committed to the interdependence of building and design." Jersey Devil architects/builders live on-site during construction of their designs, which are known for energy efficiency and innovative use of materials. Badanes has lectured on Jersey Devil's work at over 100 universities in the U.S., Canada, Mexico, and Europe. Their work has been the subject of two books: *The Jersey Devil Design/Build Book* (1985) and *Devil's Workshop: 25 Years of Jersey Devil Architecture* (1997).

At the University of Washington, Badanes holds the Howard Wright Endowed Chair and leads design/build studios that have focused on community service projects for non-profit organizations in the Seattle area. He also teaches with Professor Sergio Palleroni in the Design/Build Mexico program, which won an AIA Education Honor Award in 1997.

authors

Daniel Adams
Adams, Anderson & McClashan
San Francisco, CA

Terron Cox, Jim Olsen, Gona Grover,
Geoffrey C. Adams and Karen King
University of New Mexico School of
Architecture and Planning
Albuquerque, NM

Kenny Myers and Rustin Ostler,
Geoffrey C. Adams and Karen King
University of New Mexico School of
Architecture and Planning
Albuquerque, NM

Ian Blue, Veree Parker, Gina Pavia
Geoffrey C. Adams and Karen King
University of New Mexico School of
Architecture and Planning
Albuquerque, NM

Ryan Spruston and Sean Ahlquist
Proces2
San Francisco, CA

Bill Arens
Boulder, CO

Michele Auer
Quincy, MA

Steven Baczek
Reading, MA

Adam K. Baldwin
Scott Marek & Adam Baldwin
Dallas, TX

Scott Ball
Community Housing Resource Center and
Bloomer & Segrest Architects
Atlanta, GA

Philippe Barriere
Philippe Barriere Collective
Lawrence, KS

Jeremy J. Beaudry and Meredith Warner
Champaign, IL

Michael Becherer
Lexington, KY

John Bencich, Mike Boland and Mark Blair
Square Feet Studio
Atlanta, GA

Kurt Bennett
North Miami Beach, FL

Greg Biancardi
Biancardi Studio
South Windsor, CT

Gail Peter Borden
Borden Partnership
Raleigh, NC

Todd Boyd
Somerville, MA

Rob Bradford and Maria Perez
Gensler, Houston, TX

Jody Brantner
Page Goolrick Architecture, PC
New York, NY

Marshall Brown
Brooklyn, NY

Timothy Brown
Tim Brown Architecture &
Micaco Oshima
Asheville, NC

Kimberly Brown, Jane Greenwood and
Jason Labutka, College of Architecture
Mississippi State University
Mississippi State, MS

David D. Brown, Rebecca Sharkey, Sam
Zimmerman-Bergman, Sharon Gallant and
Tim Stauffer, Albany, CA

Jim Burton
Seattle, WA

Steve Click and Ben Butler
Team ADA
Fayetteville, AR

Anja Caldwell
Eco ipso Design
Washington, NC

Daniel H. Cantwell
DHC Design
Staten Island, NY

Chris Carson
C Squared
Bentonville, AR

Jason Chandler
Chandler & Associates
South Miami, FL

Yoon J. Choi
YCD
London, UK

Carlo E. Frugiuele, Massimo E. Marinelli
and Jason Clampet
Urban Office Architecture
New York, NY

Ronald Rose and Nazneen Cooper
Cooper Rose Design
Acton, MA

Robert Corser
Cambridge, MA

Andres Cortes and Aran Coakley
Brooklyn, NY

Paul Coughlin and Jaime Bedard
Studio BC
Philadelphia, PA

Christopher D. Crowder
Norfolk, VA

Alejandra de Diego Llopis
Stillwater, OK

Manuel Del Monte
Miami, FL

Emily Andersen and Geoffrey DeOld
New York, NY

David Dodt
Dodt/Lauterbach
Evanston, IL

David R. Dolan
Ventura, CA

Hui Du and Yiling Mackay
Gaithersburg, MD

Jeff Williams and Stephanie Dunham
College of Engineering, Architecture
and Technology, Oklahoma State University
Stillwater, OK

John Gavin Dwyer
Sala Architects
Stillwater, MN

Bill Edgerton
Charlottesville, VA

Ned Engs
Engs Architects
Los Angeles, CA

Darren D. Eryou
Eryou Engineering
Northport, NY

Teddy Falloway and Won Chang
Dale City, VA

Amy Farina Urban
Troy, NY

Ariel Fausto and Nicole Michel
New York, NY

Gabriel Feld
Cambridge, MA

Jennifer Evans and Daniel Ferrario
Chicago, IL

Harvey Ferrero
Ferndale, MI

Matthew Finn
Matthew Finn Design
Woodland Hills, CA

Carlos Fueyo
Miami, FL

Ben Gauslin
Chicago, IL

Ben Gist
Gist-Weber-Dalton
Seattle, WA

Justin Gologorsky
Boston, MA

Vinicius Gorgati
Boston, MA

Tina Govan and Tim Martin
Raleigh, NC

Leisa Graham
Cincinnati, OH

Eric Haas, Chava Danielson
and Michael Aquino
DSH
Los Angeles, CA

Scott R.J. Harada
Honolulu, HI

David M. Harmon
Denver, CO

Doug Hecker and Martha Skinner
FieldOffice
Clemson, SC

James H. Henderson
Henderson/Laverne/Strenning
Santa Rosa, CA

Roberto S. Hernandez
Ames, IA

David Hill, Matt Konar and
Elizabeth Moore
Pearce Brinkley Cease & Lee
Raleigh, NC

Jennifer Attride
PBC+L Architecture
Raleigh, NC

Sandy Hirshen and Rui Nunes
Henriquez Partners Architects
Vancouver, CANADA

Kevan Hoertdoerfer
Kevin Hoertdoerfer Architects
Charleston, SC

Christopher Hood
Boxborough, MA

Trey Hromyak
San Francisco, CA

Robert Humble and Jonathan Barriger
Robert Humble Architects
Seattle, WA

Richard Hansen
Loring Cruz Design & Consulting
Long Beach, CA

Matthew Jasion
New York, NY

Bruce Medendorp
Dan Vos Construction Company
Ada, MI

Leah Karnes and Cheryl Click
Fayetteville, AR

W. Brian Keith, Jonathan Brown,
Bob Bullis, John Schrader, Corvin Matei
and Bob James with Team Leaders
Alex Ngu and Melissa Joesoef
James, Harwick + Partners
Dallas, TX

Darren M. Kelly
Project Quest
Columbus, OH

Ann Keith Kennedy
Philadelphia, PA

William Kenworthey, Marissa Anzek,
David Evans and You-Chang Jeon
New York, NY

Mir Qamar and Andrew Kikta
Pittsburgh, PA

Nam hoon Kim
Cambridge, MA

Andy Kim and Sang Jae Lee
Fayetteville, AR

Helmina Kim
Brooklyn, NY

Jody Kinney
Miami, FL

Tanner Kirchoff
Manhattan, KS

Ilya S. Korolev
Brooklyn, NY

Matthew Kosednar
DFD Architecture, Inc.
Phoenix, AZ

Scott Krenner and Andy Saur
Duluth, MN

Motonobu Kurokawa
New York, NY

Jo Le
Stillwater, OK

Lida K. Lewis
Cincinnati, OH

Anthony Lopez
Miami, FL

Lira Luis, Chris Ilg, Navin Pathangay
and Steve Soenksen
Ilg Luis Pathangey & Soenksen Design
Phoenix, AZ

Jamie T. Malloy
Des Moines, IA

Eric McDaniel
Green Sky Design
Portland, OR

Paul McKean
Yost Grube Hall Architecture
Portland, OR

Emil Mertzel
Lookingglass Architecture & Design
Los Angeles, CA

Eric Meyerowitz and Dianne Kraus
I.D.E.A.
Santa Monica, CA

Edward Mitchell
New Haven, CT

Philip Mitropoulos
Mitropoulos Architecture
New York, NY

Jason Monteverde and Andrew Centanni
Oak Brook, IL

Benjamin Moore
Santa Fe, NM

A. Paul Moran
Moran Architects, PC
Phoenix, AZ

E. Adam Luginbill and Evonne Morales
Cincinnati, OH

John E. Morris
School of Architecture
Clemson University
Clemson, SC

Marvin Moss
Ardmore, OK

John Nelson
College of Architecture
University of North Carolina - Charlotte
Charlotte, NC

Oliver Centanni
Vancouver, CANADA

Nicholas Nye
Ocean Isle Beach, NC

Alberto J. Otero
Otero Architects
Coral Gables, FL

Philip Pankiewicz
Brooklyn, NY

Andrijana Pavlovic and Amy Garrett
Fayetteville, AR

Maggie Peng, Ada Tolla,
Giuseppe Lignano and Guy Zucker
LOT-EK Architecture
New York, NY

Mario Alexis Perez
Miami, FL

Scott Michael Perez
Fulcrum Studios, PC
Indianapolis, IN

William Petersen, Jr.
Nanjemoy, MD

Richard Pipek and Margaret Johnston
University of Wisconsin - Milwaukee
Milwaukee, WI

Tim Power
Studio Power
Milano, ITALY

Bruce L. Quigley, Todd Alwine,
Lisa D. Iulo, Dan Mayer, Kim Patten,
Maria Vera and Shai Yeshayahu
Seven B
Harrisburg, PA

Billy Quimby
Quimby & Sayigh
San Francisco, CA

Scott C. Radcliff
School of Architecture
Clemson University
Clemson, SC

Juan C. Ricardes
Tampa, FL

William T. Ricket
Marc Bailey-William Ricket Architecture
Niskayuna, NY

Evan Ripley
House Collective
New York, NY

Jonah Ritter
Minneapolis , MN

W. Douglas Romines
Schwartz Architects
New York, NY

George Roushakes
Pulse3am
New York, NY

William T. Ruhl
Boston, MA

Philip Rusk
University of Arkansas
Fayetteville, AR

Jack Ryan
Providence, RI

Ruben Santos
San Francisco, CA

Elizabeth Derr and Eric Sauda
Becky/Bill/Robby/Jedidiah Gant/Liz
Charlotte, NC

Silas Seger
Manhattan, KS

Douglas R. Seidler
Cambridge, MA

Eric R. Shamp
Redlands, CA

Nicole Cannon and Huay Wee
Marmol Radziner & Associates
Los Angeles, CA

Jeff Williams and Scott Smardo
College of Engineering, Architecture
and Technology, Oklahoma State
University
Stillwater, OK

Chad Stith
San Francisco, CA

Benjamin R. Spencer
Gerich/Spencer
Charlottesville, VA

Bannavis Andrew Sribyatta and
Damian Ponton
FLUX-Los Angeles & Miami, FL
Los Angeles, CA

Jeremy Martin Strawn
Fayetteville, AR

Patrick Stuart
Columbus, OH

Jason Stucker
Manhattan, KS

Dan Stuver
Alexandria, VA

Marc Swackhamer (School of
Architecture & Interior Design,
University of Cincinnati,) and
Blair Satterfield (Bricker + Canady
Architects & Rice University – Houston)
with Consultants, Robert Burnham
(University of Cincinnati) and Cory
Satterfield (Flad and Associates, Madison)
Team Name: sleeve
Cincinnati, OH

SiJing Tan
Los Angeles, CA

Lisa Tilder
Knowlton School of Architecture
Ohio State University
Columbus, OH

Alastair Townsend
Des Moines, IA

Tat Chan and Alexia Valentine
VIA Concepts, Inc.
Neptune Beach, FL

Erin Vali and Roy Leone with
Andrew Deibel
Ulterior Mode LLC
Brooklyn, NY

Roberto Ventura
Richmond, VA

Robert Viergutz
Rosenzweig & Viergutz
Phoenix, AZ

Gabe Vogl
Manhattan, KS

Cass Calder Smith and Aaron Maret
CCS Architecture
San Francisco, CA

Kevin Wagstaff and Mary Cerrone
Cerrone and Wagstaff Architects
Pittsburgh, PA

Glenn Waguespack and
Adam Wilbrecht
Minneapolis, MN

Ralph Jonathan Walker
Sherman Oaks, CA

Edward Wansing
Marshall, MO

David Wanzer
Oklahoma City, OK

Philip Ward
Stillwater, OK

Jeff Williams and Yulis Wardjiman
College of Engineering,
Architecture and Technology,
Oklahoma State University
Stillwater, OK

Valerie Wersinger
Seattle, WA

Allan Wexler
New York, NY

Joseph Xiong
College of Architecture,
Planning and Design
Kansas State University
Manhattan, KS

Shinya Yamada, Juan Calaf and
Peter Aeschbacher
Los Angeles, CA

Dwight Yee
Pittsburgh, PA

Travis Young
Studio Momentum Architecture
Austin, TX

Jennifer Siegal
Office of Mobile Design
Venice, CA

Miljan Radonjic and
Aleksander Jovanovic
Radonjic & Partners
Pancevo SERBIA & MONTENEGRO

Note: More than 442 design proposals were received for the project and we were unable to list all of the participants due to the length of this publication. SECCA wishes to gratefully acknowledge all of the participants who entered.

List of
SECCA Staff

SECCA is supported by The Arts Council of Winston-Salem and Forsyth County, and the North Carolina Arts Council, an agency funded by the State of North Carolina and the National Endowment for the Arts.